Our Own
Thing

Our Own Thing

Contemporary Thought in Poetry

edited by
GRETCHEN B. CRAFTS

Department of English
California State University, San Diego

PRENTICE-HALL, INC.
Englewood Cliffs, New Jersey

Library of Congress Cataloging in Publication Data

CRAFTS, GRETCHEN   comp.
  Our own thing.

  (English literature series)
  1. Poetry, Modern. I. Title.
PN6101.C68   808.81   72–6468
ISBN 0-13-644468-7

PRENTICE-HALL ENGLISH LITERATURE SERIES

Maynard Mack, Editor

Printed in the United States of America

10 9 8 7 6 5 4 3 2 1

Prentice-Hall International, Inc., *London*
Prentice-Hall of Australia, Pty. Ltd., *Sydney*
Prentice-Hall of Canada, Ltd., *Toronto*
Prentice-Hall of India Private Limited, *New Delhi*
Prentice-Hall of Japan, Inc., *Tokyo*

ACKNOWLEDGMENTS

"Mirror" by permission of Karen Nurmi, student, San Diego State College, 1969.
"How still the hawk" from *Seeing Is Believing*, © 1960 by Astor-Honor, Inc. Reprinted by permission of Astor-Honor, Inc., Stamford, Conn. 06904.
"Amidst the Reddening Forest" reprinted by permission of Vytas Dukas.
"Time Past" by permission of D. A. Stahl, from *Bravura* (Palomar College, 1967).
"The Lady and the Physician" © 1961 by Anthony Ostroff. Reprinted from his volume *Imperatives* by permission of Harcourt Brace Jovanovich, Inc.
"Viewpoints" reprinted by permission of Susan Murray, from *Bravura* (Palomar College, 1967).

Acknowledgments

"Evacuee" by permission of T. J. Freeman, student, Palomar College, 1970.

"He Always Wanted To" reprinted from *The Journal*, Paul H. Sherry, editor, VIII, No. 1 (October 1969), page 11.

"When Sometimes" by permission of Mary Lou Denman McIlwaine, student, University of California at San Diego, 1966.

"On an Ecdysiast" reprinted from John Ciardi, *This Strangest Everything* (New Brunswick, N.J.: Rutgers University Press, 1966).

"Past Midnight" reprinted by permission of Vytas Dukas.

"My Goblet" by permission of Blair H. Allen, student, San Diego State College, 1969.

"The Love Song of J. Alfred Prufrock" from *Collected Poems 1909–1962* by T. S. Eliot, copyright, 1936, by Harcourt Brace Jovanovich, Inc.; copyright 1963, 1964, by T. S. Eliot. Reprinted by permission of Harcourt Brace Jovanovich, Inc., and Faber and Faber Ltd.

"Misconception" by permission of Bonnie Buchanan, from *Las Obras* (Vista High School, 1969).

"Old Smell Carpets" by permission of Michael Pogliano, student, University of Colorado, 1969.

"Eleanor Rigby" copyright © 1966 Northern Songs Limited. Used by permission. All rights reserved.

"The Big I" reprinted by permission of Charles Scribner's Sons from *The Gardener and Other Poems* by John Hall Wheelock. Copyright © 1961 John Hall Wheelock.

"For a Friend" reprinted by permission of Charles Scribner's Sons from *For Love* by Robert Creeley. Copyright © 1962 Robert Creeley.

"Fascination" by permission of Pat Folk, from *Bravura* (Palomar College, 1966).

"To a Mad Friend" from *The Breaking of the Day* by Peter Davison. © by Peter Davison. Reprinted by permission of Yale University Press.

"These Lives" copyright © 1966 by Harvey Shapiro. Reprinted from *Battle Report*, by Harvey Shapiro, by permission of Wesleyan University Press.

"Erewhon" reprinted by permission from Eliot Glassheim, *The Restless Giant* (Cerillos, N.M.: San Marcos Press, 1968).

"To Smith" by permission of Barbara Miles, student, San Diego State College, 1969.

"Walking" by permission of Betsy Richards, from *Las Obras* (Vista High School, 1969).

"Mirror, Mirror" by permission of Bonnie Buchanan, from *Las Obras* (Vista High School, 1969).

"The Treehouse" by permission of James Emanuel.

"Lucy in the Sky with Diamonds" copyright © 1967 Northern Songs Limited. Used by permission. All rights reserved.

"Call It a Good Marriage" reprinted by permission of Collins-Knowlton-Wing, Inc. Copyright © 1961 Robert Graves.

"Out of Tune" from *The Breaking of the Day* by Peter Davison. © by Peter Davison. Reprinted by permission of Yale University Press.

"March" from *The Complete Poems and Selected Letters and Prose of Hart Crane*. Copyright renewed 1963 by Liveright Publishing Corp., New York. Reprinted by permission of the publisher.

"Discrimination" from Kenneth Rexroth, *Collected Shorter Poems*. Copyright 1949 by Kenneth Rexroth. Reprinted by permission of New Directions Publishing Corporation.

"Out, Out—" from *The Poetry of Robert Frost* edited by Edward Connery Lathem. Copyright 1916, © 1969 by Holt, Rinehart and Winston, Inc. Copyright 1944 by Robert Frost. Reprinted by permission of Holt, Rinehart and Winston, Inc.

"Cast Up" from Lawrence Ferlinghetti, *A Coney Island of the Mind*. Copyright © 1958 by Lawrence Ferlinghetti. Reprinted by permission of New Directions Publishing Corporation.

"Bad Dog" by permission of Barbara Miles, student, San Diego State College, 1969.

"The Pennycandystore Beyond the El" from Lawrence Ferlinghetti, *A Coney Island of the Mind*. Copyright © 1958 by Lawrence Ferlinghetti. Reprinted by permission of New Directions Publishing Corporation.

"Past Time" copyright © 1964 by Harvey Shapiro. Reprinted from *Battle Report*, by Harvey Shapiro, by permission of Wesleyan University Press.

"The Moment" copyright © 1963 by Beatrice Roethke as Administratrix to the Estate of Theodore Roethke from *The Collected Poems of Theodore Roethke*. Reprinted by permission of Doubleday & Company, Inc.

"Invasion" by permission of Blair H. Allen, student, San Diego State College, 1970.

"Picture of a Nude in a Machine Shop" from William Carlos Williams, *Collected Later Poems*. Copyright 1934 by William Carlos Williams. Reprinted by permission of New Directions Publishing Corporation.

"A Plea" reprinted from John Ciardi, *In the Stoneworks* (New Brunswick, N.J.: Rutgers University Press, 1962).

"Girl" by permission of Barbara Miles, student, San Diego State College, 1969.

"The Warning" reprinted by permission of Charles Scribner's Sons from *For Love* by Robert Creeley. Copyright © 1962 Robert Creeley.

Acknowledgments

"And She Waiting" from *Views of Jeopardy* by Jack Gilbert. Copyright © 1962 by Yale University. Reprinted by permission of Yale University Press.

"Raped" by permission of Stuart Polzin, student, Palomar College, 1970.

"in heavenly realms" © 1963 by Marion Morehouse Cummings. Reprinted from *73 Poems* by E. E. Cummings by permission of Harcourt Brace Jovanovich, Inc.

"Letter to My Sister" by permission of Anne Spencer.

"Yesterday" by permission of Michael Pogliano, student, University of Colorado, 1969.

"I Think It Was Because You Laughed" by permission of Sharon Buck, student, San Diego State College, 1969.

"Erat Hora" from Ezra Pound, *Personae*. Copyright 1926 by Ezra Pound. Reprinted by permission of New Directions Publishing Corporation.

"Memories" reprinted by permission of Catherine Cho Woo.

"Goodbye" from *The Breaking of the Day* by Peter Davison. © by Peter Davison. Reprinted by permission of Yale University Press.

"The Waste Land" from *Collected Poems 1809–1962* by T. S. Eliot, copyright, 1936, by Harcourt Brace Jovanovich, Inc., copyright 1963, 1964 by T. S. Eliot. Reprinted by permission of Harcourt Brace Jovanovich, Inc. and Faber and Faber Ltd.

"Auto Wreck" copyright 1942 and renewed 1970 by Karl Shapiro. From *Selected Poems*, by Karl Shapiro. Reprinted by permission of Random House, Inc.

"next to of course god" copyright, 1926, by Horace Liveright; copyright, 1954, by E. E. Cummings. By permission of Harcourt Brace Jovanovich, Inc.

"To My Mother" reprinted from *Collected Poems 1930 to 1965* by George Barker. Copyright © 1957, 1962 and 1965 by George Granville Barker. Reprinted by permission of October House Inc.

"A Cold Front" from William Carlos Williams, *Collected Later Poems*. Copyright 1948 by William Carlos Williams. Reprinted by permission of New Directions Publishing Corporation.

"Deep Inside Wallet" by permission of Scott Kinney, student, San Diego State College, 1969.

"There Are Many Trades" reprinted by permission of Vytas Dukas.

"The Common Life" copyright 1942 by Wallace Stevens and renewed 1970 by Holly Stevens Stephenson. From *Collected Poems of Wallace Stevens*. Reprinted by permission of Alfred A. Knopf, Inc.

"San Juan" by permission of Michael Pogliano, student, University of Colorado, 1969.

"The Story of Isaac" copyright © 1967, 1969 Stranger Music, Inc. Used by permission. All rights reserved.

"Morning at the Window" from *Collected Poems 1909–1962* by T. S. Eliot, copyright, 1936 by Harcourt Brace Jovanovich, Inc., copyright 1963, 1964 by T. S. Eliot. Reprinted by permission of Harcourt Brace Jovanovich, Inc. and Faber and Faber Ltd.

"Canción de las Hormigas" reprinted by permission of Grove Press, Inc. Copyright © 1967 by Paul Blackburn.

"The Maze" by permission of Blair H. Allen, student, San Diego State College, 1969.

"Southern Mansion" reprinted by permission of Harold Ober Associates Incorporated. Copyright © 1963 by Arna Bontemps.

"Niggertown" reprinted by permission of Charles Scribner's Sons from *A Stone, A Leaf, A Door* by Thomas Wolfe. Copyright 1945 Maxwell Perkins, Executor Administrator of Estate of Thomas Wolfe.

"A Housewife Looks at the Poor" reprinted by permission of Bert Almon from *The Return and Other Poems* (San Marcos Press, 1968).

"Juvenile Hall" by permission of Sharon Buck, student, San Diego State College, 1969.

"Corner" reprinted with permission of The Macmillan Company, from *In the Financial District* by Ralph Pomeroy. Copyright © by Ralph Pomeroy, 1961.

"In Order To" from Kenneth Patchen, *Collected Poems*. Copyright 1954 by Kenneth Patchen. Reprinted by permission of New Directions Publishing Corporation.

"Malcolm X, Talking to the City" reprinted from *Quickly Aging Here: Some Poets of the 1970's*, edited by Geof Hewitt (© Doubleday & Company, Inc., New York, 1969).

"Harlem" copyright 1948 by Alfred A. Knopf, Inc. From *The Panther and the Lash*, by Langston Hughes. Reprinted by permission of the publisher.

"The Hard Sell" reprinted from John Ciardi, *This Strangest Everything* (New Brunswick, N.J.: Rutgers University Press, 1966).

"Salutation" from Ezra Pound, *Personae*. Copyright 1926 by Ezra Pound. Reprinted by permission of New Directions Publishing Corporation.

"from pigeons to people" by permission of Alfred K. Weber, student, San Diego State College, 1969.

"On Roman Traffic" reprinted from John Ciardi, *This Strangest Everything* (New Brunswick, N.J.: Rutgers University Press, 1966).

"A Fire-Truck" © 1958 by Richard Wilbur. Reprinted from his volume *Advice to a Prophet and Other Poems* by permission of Harcourt Brace Jovanovich, Inc. First published in *The New Yorker*.

Acknowledgments

"The Soul of Youth—The Fear of Age" by permission of Sharon Sosna, student, San Diego State College, 1970.

"While My Guitar Gently Weeps" copyright © 1968, 1969 Harrisongs Music, Inc. Written by George Harrison. Used by permission. All rights reserved. International Copyright secured.

"The Fall of Rome" copyright 1947 by W. H. Auden. From *Collected Shorter Poems 1927–1957*, by W. H. Auden. Reprinted by permission of Random House, Inc.

"Long-Legged Fly" reprinted with permission of The Macmillan Company from *Collected Poems* by William Butler Yeats. Copyright 1940 by Georgie Yeats, renewed 1968 by Bertha Georgie Yeats, Michael Butler Yeats and Anne Yeats. By permission of Macmillan Company of Canada Ltd. and Mr. M. B. Yeats.

"Accomplishment" by permission of Bonnie Buchanan, from *Las Obras* (Vista High School, 1969).

"The Emancipation of George-Hector" reprinted by permission of Mari E. Evans from *I Am a Black Woman*, published by William Morrow and Company, 1970.

"Earth" reprinted by permission of Charles Scribner's Sons from *The Gardener and Other Poems* by John Hall Wheelock. Copyright © 1961 John Hall Wheelock.

"Ambition" from *A Bowl of Bishop* by Morris Bishop. Copyright 1954 by Morris Bishop. Reprinted by permission of the publisher, The Dial Press. Originally published in *The New Yorker*.

"Leda and the Swan" reprinted with permission of The Macmillan Company from *Collected Poems* by William Butler Yeats. Copyright 1928 by The Macmillan Company, renewed 1956 by Georgie Yeats. By permission of the Macmillan Company of Canada Ltd. and Mr. M. B. Yeats.

"With God on Our Side" © 1963 M. Witmark & Sons. All rights reserved. Used by permission of Warner Bros. Music.

"Crystal Night" reprinted from John Ciardi, *This Strangest Everything* (New Brunswick, N.J.: Rutgers University Press, 1966).

"The Dead" reprinted with permission of The Macmillan Company from *No Gods Are False* by Augustine Bowe. Copyright © by Julia Bowe, 1968.

"The Light on the Pewter Dish" from Kenneth Rexroth, *Collected Shorter Poems*. Copyright 1949 by Kenneth Rexroth. Reprinted by permission of New Directions Publishing Corporation.

"Anthem for Doomed Youth" from Wilfred Owen, *Collected Poems*, edited by C. Day Lewis. Copyright Chatto & Windus, Ltd. 1946, © 1963. Reprinted by permission of New Directions Publishing Corporation, the Estate of the late Harold Owen, and Chatto & Windus, Ltd.

"Children in the Shelter" reprinted with permission of The Macmillan Company from *Night Flight to Hanoi* by Daniel Berrigan, S.J. Copyright © 1968 by Daniel Berrigan, S.J.

"Fish" reprinted with permission of The Macmillan Company from *False Gods, Real Men* by Daniel Berrigan, S.J. Copyright © 1969 by Daniel Berrigan, S.J.

"The War Is Here" by permission of Blair H. Allen, student, San Diego State College, 1969.

"Dulce et Decorum Est" from Wilfred Owen, *Collected Poems*, edited by C. Day Lewis. Copyright Chatto & Windus, Ltd. 1946, © 1963. Reprinted by permission of New Directions Publishing Corporation, the Estate of the late Harold Owen, and Chatto & Windus, Ltd.

"The Initiation Rites at Mylai" by permission of Barbara Miles, student, San Diego State College, 1969.

"The End" by permission of Miles Weaver, student, San Diego State College, 1970.

"Louse Hunting" by permission of Chatto & Windus, Ltd. and the Author's Literary Estate, and by permission of Schocken Books Inc. from *Collected Poems* by Isaac Rosenberg. Copyright © 1949 by Schocken Books Inc.

"It's Not Like Killing Men" by permission of Pat Folk, from *Bravura* (Palomar College, 1967).

"Survival: Infantry" from George Oppen, *The Materials*. Copyright © 1962 by George Oppen. Reprinted by permission of New Directions Publishing Corporation and San Francisco Review.

"The Man He Killed" reprinted with permission of The Macmillan Company from *Collected Poems* by Thomas Hardy. Copyright 1925 by The Macmillan Company. Also by permission of the Trustees of the Hardy Estate; Macmillan London & Basingstoke, and the Macmillan Company of Canada Limited.

"The War" by permission of Alfred K. Weber, student, San Diego State College, 1969.

"Ozymandias" from George Oppen, *The Materials*. Copyright © 1962 by George Oppen. Reprinted by permission of New Directions Publishing Corporation and San Francisco Review.

"One Step, After Step" by permission of George Langston, student, San Diego State College, 1969.

"I'm Dead" by permission of Sharon Buck, student, San Diego State College, 1969.

"Death" from William Carlos Williams, *Collected Later Poems*. Copyright 1934, 1944, 1948 by William Carlos Williams. Reprinted by permission of New Directions Publishing Corporation.

"Obit" reprinted with permission of The Macmillan Company from *False Gods, Real Men* by Daniel Berrigan, S.J. Copyright © 1969 by Daniel Berrigan, S.J.

"Colloquy" reprinted by permission of Charles Scribner's Sons from *The Gardener and Other Poems* by John Hall Wheelock. Copyright © 1961 John Hall Wheelock.

"Death" reprinted with permission of The Macmillan Company from *False Gods, Real Men* by Daniel Berrigan, S.J. Copyright © 1969 by Daniel Berrigan, S.J.

vii

Acknowledgments

"Elegy" copyright © 1955 by The New Republic, Inc. Reprinted by permission of Doubleday & Company, Inc.

"Aunt Helen" from *Collected Poems 1909–1962* by T. S. Eliot, copyright, 1936, by Harcourt Brace Jovanovich, Inc.; copyright © 1963, 1964, by T. S. Eliot. Reprinted by permission of Harcourt Brace Jovanovich, Inc. and Faber and Faber Ltd.

"Not Forgotten .2. Dream" from *The Breaking of the Day* by Peter Davison. © by Peter Davison. Reprinted by permission of Yale University Press.

"The Little One" reprinted from John Ciardi, *In the Stoneworks* (New Brunswick, N.J.: Rutgers University Press, 1962).

"Father's Face" by permission of Alfred K. Weber, student, San Diego State College, 1969.

"The Tag" reprinted by permission of Bert Almon from *The Return and Other Poems* (San Marcos Press, 1968).

"Elegy V" reprinted with permission of The Macmillan Company from *No Gods Are False* by Augustine Bowe. Copyright © by Julia Bowe, 1968.

"Who Killed Davey Moore?" © 1964 M. Witmark & Sons. All rights reserved. Used by permission of Warner Bros. Music.

"ABC of Culture" copyright © 1962 by Harvey Shapiro. Reprinted from *Battle Report*, by Harvey Shapiro, by permission of Wesleyan University Press.

"The Rebel" reprinted by permission of Mari E. Evans from *I Am a Black Woman*, published by William Morrow and Company, 1970.

"Musée des Beaux Arts" copyright 1940 and renewed 1968 by W. H. Auden. From *Collected Shorter Poems 1927–1957*, by W. H. Auden. Reprinted by permission of Random House, Inc. and Faber and Faber Ltd.

"The Immigrant's Wake and Requiem" by permission of the University of Chicago Press from *In Praise of Adam* by Reuel Denny. Copyright © 1961 by The University of Chicago Press.

"Dies Irae" reprinted with permission of The Macmillan Company from *No Gods Are False* by Augustine Bowe. Copyright © by Julia Bowe, 1941, 1968.

"Homage to Quintus Septimius Florentis Christianus" from Ezra Pound, *Personae*. Copyright 1926 by Ezra Pound. Reprinted by permission of New Directions Publishing Corporation.

"Peter Quince at the Clavier" copyright 1923 and renewed 1951 by Wallace Stevens. From *Collected Poems of Wallace Stevens*. Reprinted by permission of Alfred A. Knopf, Inc.

"The Man with the Blue Guitar" copyright 1936 by Wallace Stevens and renewed 1964 by Elsie Stevens and Holly Stevens. From *Collected Poems of Wallace Stevens*. Reprinted by permission of Alfred A. Knopf, Inc.

"The Proud Tree Tosses" by permission of Frank Mezta, student, San Diego State College, 1969.

"Beagles" reprinted from John Ciardi, *In the Stoneworks* (New Brunswick, N.J.: Rutgers University Press, 1962).

"What the Witch Said" copyright © 1963 by Harvey Shapiro. Reprinted from *Battle Report*, by Harvey Shapiro, by permission of Wesleyan University Press.

"warty bliggens the toad" from *archy & mehitabel* by Don Marquis. Copyright 1927 by Doubleday & Company, Inc. Reprinted by permission of the publisher.

"Hunger" from *The Breaking of the Day* by Peter Davison. © by Peter Davison. Reprinted by permission of Yale University Press.

"An Tzu" reprinted by permission of Catherine Cho Woo.

"Mongol in Kracow" reprinted by permission of Vytas Dukas.

"A Small Boy in Church" by permission of Robert Sheppard, student, Vista High School, 1969.

"Dialogue After Bishop Berkeley" reprinted by permission of Charles Scribner's Sons from *The Gardener and Other Poems* by John Hall Wheelock. Copyright © 1961 John Hall Wheelock.

"$E = MC^2$" from *A Bowl of Bishop* by Morris Bishop. Copyright 1954 by Morris Bishop. Reprinted by permission of the publisher, The Dial Press. Originally published in *The New Yorker*.

"Agnostic?" by permission of Pat Folk, from *Bravura* (Palomar College, 1966).

"Kid Stuff" by permission of Frank Horne.

"Yet Do I Marvel" from *On These I Stand* by Countee Cullen. Copyright 1925 by Harper & Row, Publishers, Inc.; renewed 1953 by Ida M. Cullen. Reprinted by permission of Harper & Row, Publishers, Inc.

"Heaven" reprinted by permission of McClelland & Stewart and of Dodd, Mead & Company, Inc. from *The Collected Poems of Rupert Brooke*. Copyright 1915 by Dodd, Mead & Company; copyright renewed 1943 by Edward Marsh.

"A Theological Definition" from George Oppen, *Of Being Numerous*. First published in *Poetry*. Copyright © 1967 by George Oppen. Reprinted by permission of New Directions Publishing Corporation.

"The Second Coming" reprinted with permission of The Macmillan Company from *Collected Poems* by William Butler Yeats. Copyright 1924 by The Macmillan Company, renewed 1952 by Bertha Georgie Yeats. By permission of The Macmillan Company of Canada Ltd. and Mr. M. B. Yeats.

Acknowledgments

"They Were Putting Up the Statue" from Lawrence Ferlinghetti, *A Coney Island of the Mind*. Copyright © 1958 by Lawrence Ferlinghetti. Reprinted by permission of New Directions Publishing Corporation.

"Jan Hus" reprinted by permission of Vytas Dukas.

"The Crucifix" reprinted with permission of The Macmillan Company from *No Gods Are False* by Augustine Bowe. Copyright © by Julia Bowe, 1941, 1968.

"God Said if You Would Not Love Me" by permission of Sharon Buck, student, San Diego State College, 1969.

"On Being Nothing" by permission of W. Scott Miller, student, Vista High School, 1969.

"See It Was Like This" from Lawrence Ferlinghetti, *A Coney Island of the Mind*. Copyright © 1958 by Lawrence Ferlinghetti. Reprinted by permission of New Directions Publishing Corporation.

Stanza from "Hugh Selwyn Mauberly" from Ezra Pound, *Personae*. Copyright 1926 by Ezra Pound. Reprinted by permission of New Directions Publishing Corporation.

Word definitions reprinted with permission from *Webster's New World Dictionary*, 2nd College Edition, David B. Guralnik, editor (Cleveland: World Publishing Company, 1970).

Contents

1 Man and Himself, 1

Contents

2 Poetry and Perception, 30

3 Man and the Other Sex, 40

Contents

4 Poetry, Subject, and Diction, 68

5 Man and the Establishment, 78

Contents

8 Poetry and Cadence, 132

9 Man and Death, 144

10 Poetry and Melody, 159

Contents

11 Man and the Gods, 171

Preface

Many poetry anthologies begin with the assumption that the average student dislikes poetry and attempt to remedy the situation by promoting better understanding of how a poem works. The theory is that people who dislike poetry do not understand it. While this theory may contain some truth, it fails to consider one very important fact: although many young people may profess to hate poetry, they are almost without exception extremely fond of poetry in one form or another. One need only listen closely to the lyrics screeched to the accompaniment of twanging guitars over countless radios across any campus to verify the truth of this statement. Some of these lyrics, most of which were written by persons close to the ages of college students, and some even written by students themselves, are as worthy of being called poetry as many lyrics recognized as such by scholars. This book, then, begins with the assumption that virtually all college students like poetry.

Another common fallacy is that undergraduates are incapable of understanding modern poetry. On the contrary, modern poetry—that is, poetry that is "modern" in spirit—is exactly what students do understand and enjoy. Instead of including much of the poetry that they have already met in high school, I have attempted in this text to present poems that are new to students—and in many cases to teachers as well—and that are "modern." This does not mean that I have excluded great poems from the past, however; many contemporary problems are both timely and timeless (sex, for example). But minimizing obsolete ideas is one goal of this text. In an attempt to achieve this goal, the book also includes works of popular artists, well-known and lesser-known modern poets, and student poets.

Because poetry deals with man, his world, and the relationship between the two, six chapters of this book deal with man and his most pressing problems: Man and Himself, Man and the Other Sex, Man and the Establishment, Man and War, Man and Death, and Man and the Gods. Between each of these chapters is a discussion of how poems work: Poetry and Perception; Poetry, Subject, and Diction; Poetry and Image; Poetry and Cadence; and Poetry and Melody. This dual arrangement should enable the student to study poetry with flexibility. For example, chapters dealing with man's relationship to his universe can be studied for meaning and social significance alone or coordinated with chapters on poetic technique to give a broader understanding of poetry as art. Chapters on poetic technique can be ignored, touched upon lightly, or delved into deeply, depending on the whim of the instructor or the dedication of the student. The poems themselves have been selected with both types of interest in mind, and perhaps even more important, with attention to the ideas now spreading across college campuses throughout the country. Those ideas are argued in bull sessions, discussed in classes, and in recent years screamed over bullhorns at college presidents. The establishment, war, death, God, sex, and, most important of all, himself—young people everywhere are meeting these ideas head-on. These are the topics of *Our Own Thing.*

Acknowledgment must be made to those without whose cooperation and stoic forbearance this book would never have survived its birth: members of the Prentice-Hall staff; members of the California State College at San Diego English Department's office staff, Louis Thomason, Clara Andrews, Genevieve Tigner, Mary Huntley, and Virginia Martin, who have helped in innumerable ways; my colleagues, Ruth Brown, Harriet Haskell, Ruth Dirks, Mary Denman, and Shirley Sykes, who have suffered through my incessant typing and technical questions, all the while giving their moral support; Ed Newton, who helped with last-minute details; my students, who have suffered while I experimented to find just the right combination of poems; my family, who have endured my unorthodox hours, exasperating preoccupation, and countless TV dinners; my parents, who taught me to persevere; and Virginia Haven, whose incredible courage in the face of insurmountable odds has been a sustaining inspiration—had I only finished in time for her to know.

Special thanks must go to the following students from all over the country who contributed poetry: Karen Nurmi, D. A. Stahl, Susan Murray, T. J. Freeman, Mary Lou Denman, Blair H. Allen, Bonnie Buchanan, Michael Pogliano, Pat Folk, Barbara Miles, Betsy Richards, Stuart Kent Polzin, Sharon Buck, Scott Kinney, Alfred K. Weber, Sharon Sosna, Miles Weaver, George Langston, Bill Miller, Frank Mezta, and Robert Sheppard.

Our Own
Thing

1
Man
and Himself

MIRROR
KAREN NURMI

Can the reflection
from your shining surface tell
these thoughts to others?

Although introspection is by no means a new phenomenon,
today's increasingly chaotic universe has caused us to look within our-
selves perhaps more than man has done at any other time in history. Self-
examination is particularly strong during the early adult years of our
lives. "Who am I? What am I? What will become of me?" Such questions
often cross our minds. The answers to them, however, too often remain
both elusive and illusive, which only adds to our inner tension, causing
us sometimes to search deeper for answers, and sometimes to despair at
our "identity crisis."

Many recently popular songs deal with identity crises—John Lennon
and Paul McCartney's "Eleanor Rigby," for instance, and Judy Collins's
"Albatross." Likewise, many poets, both past and present, have examined
the problem of search for self.

Poetry, in fact, is for several reasons the ideal vehicle for conveying
man's innermost feelings about himself. Saying the most in the fewest
possible words, poetry condenses thoughts, vividly spotlighting only the
most important elements of experience in a way that no other form of
literature does. Consider the following lines, first as they were originally
written and then as they might appear in ordinary prose:

How still the hawk
Hangs innocent above
Its native wood:
Distance, that purifies the act
Of all intent, has graced
Intent with beauty.

In the distance I see a hawk that seems to be hanging in one spot above the forest where it lives. Although the hawk probably intends to dive upon and devour a hapless victim, from this distance his anticipated violence seems (as all evil intents seem from a distance) to have a certain beauty about it.

The prose rendering gives the same information about the hawk and what it represents as the poem; but there the similarity ends. Not only is the wonder—perhaps even the amazement—of the viewer lost in translation from poetry to prose, but thirty-three extra words are necessary to cover the same detail!

A second reason why poetry works so well to convey innermost feelings is that poetry is primarily concerned with the area of experience, and most good poetry presents *universal experience*—experience that remains basically unchanged from age to age. Even if we have no first-hand knowledge of such experience, we have read or heard about it. In perhaps the most widely known lines of poetry ever written, for example, Hamlet struggled almost four hundred years ago with an eternal problem: whether to take the easy path and allow fate to dictate to him, or to battle along the more difficult route and attempt to direct fate:

To be, or not to be: that is the question:
Whether 'tis nobler in the mind to suffer
The slings and arrows of outrageous fortune,
Or to take arms against a sea of troubles,
And by opposing end them . . . ?

A third reason why poetry makes such a fine vehicle for conveying one's self-image and self-doubt is that it can capture the reader as no other literature can. Reading poetry involves the total person. Most of what we read in college involves the intellect alone. Reading and understanding poetry, however, enmeshes us in a fourfold experience involving intellect, senses, emotions, and imagination.

It is no wonder, then, that contemporary writers who wish to be intensely introspective tend to choose poetry as their literary form. Most of their poems, which perhaps indicates today's tension-ridden times, cry out for recognition of self in a world where human identity is too often a faceless IBM card of neatly arranged square-punched holes. The search for identity is the general theme of the poems in this section. In some of them self is unconsciously revealed by the speaker, as in Browning's "My Last Duchess." In others there is simply recognition of a fact of life, as in D. A. Stahl's "Time Past." But too often a feeble cry for acceptance penetrates a bleak reality, as in "He Always Wanted To."

AMIDST THE REDDENING FOREST

LEONID MARTYNOV

(Translated by Vytas Dukas)

Amidst
The crackling
Black branches
Mumbling:
—"What does he want?"—   5
I wander exhausted
And the rain soaks and soaks and soaks.
And the branches,
With their bending claws
Almost stab my eyes;   10
They do not design their own grandeur
And yet I feel so humble.
The curtain of leaves,
Leaves me behind,
Amidst the reddening forest   15
I become more and more visible.

TIME PAST

D. A. STAHL

I learned to breathe sunshine
and see through amber,
Hear sorrow as joy sounds
and taste happiness,
Smell fresh rain in a world   5
of searing deserts,
Touch the velvetness of life
while holding death,

3

Feel like laughter when tears
    fall with blood,   10
Catch and hold song others
    couldn't stay.
But age seasons illusion
    and colors it—gray.

What effect is produced by *paradox* (contradiction)?
State the *theme* (central idea) of the poem.
How does the final statement of the poem coincide with your observations?

THE LADY AND THE PHYSICIAN

ANTHONY OSTROFF

"I want to feel well. I've come to you."
"What seems to be the trouble?" the doctor said.
The lady removed her gloves, unpinned
Her hat, and then let down the red, red

Tress of her hair. "I cannot hear,"   5
She said, "if the sun speaks to me, or the flowers.
Job died old and full of days.
I fear that I shall die full of hours."

"Do you think they speak?" he asked. "I do
Not know," she said. "I see, I taste the air,   10
It's clear they should." "Why?" said the doctor.
"Why?" she echoed. She thought he was unfair.

As if anyone could say *why!* What
Kept the earth from speaking, if it did not,
Or her from hearing, if it did,   15
That was the question. "I'm sorry, my dear. I forgot

Myself," the doctor smiled. "You came
For professional care. Follow this to the letter.
Here." He wrote on a slip of paper.
The lady felt immediately better.   20

She tucked her hair, the color of sun
And flowers she could not hear, under the new
Blue of her hat, smoothed on her gloves,
And that was that. "Thank you," she said. "Thank you."

And when she was gone the doctor thought   25
On science, so much like beauty, so inexact,
The marvelous form of πr^2
Which never worked out but was a matter of fact.

What is the significance of Job?
What is the significance of what the lady cannot hear?
How do she and the doctor relate to your world?
How does the final stanza relate to the rest of the poem?
Compare and contrast this poem to "Time Past."

VIEWPOINTS

SUSAN MURRAY

I forget the man who always slept
The stars away—he never knew that they
Were there to lift the human heart—his
Little world was circumscribed by day.

I will forget the man who grouped the stars   5
By magnitudes—to him the Pleiades
Were points upon galactic latitudes
Which he precisely analyzed for me.

But how shall I forget the quiet man
Who gave me starry diadems to keep   10
Because he left so many things unsaid
When there were stars enough to make me weep.

What kind of man is described in stanza I? In stanza II? In stanza III?
What are *starry diadems?* What do they suggest?
Why did the "quiet man" of the third stanza have significance for the
speaker? What does this significance imply beyond the poem?

EVACUEE

T. J. FREEMAN

Whispering from without, one day
found him in, anew
and asked him if he couldn't say
what he was to do

Whispering his reply would be   5
fully free from doubt
Only if he too could see
inside from without

Whispering from without, lately
found that he got out   10
having himself decided to be
whispering from without.

Compare and contrast this poem with the preceding three.
What is suggested by the juxtaposition between *in* and *without?*

INFANT SORROW

WILLIAM BLAKE

My mother groaned! my father wept.
Into the dangerous world I leapt:
Helpless, naked, piping loud:
Like a fiend hid in a cloud.

Struggling in my father's hands,   5
Striving against my swaddling bands,
Bound and weary I thought best
To sulk upon my mother's breast.

Carefully consider the language of "Infant Sorrow." What do such
words as *dangerous, fiend,* and *struggling* suggest?
Notice the progression from *leapt* to *sulk.* What does this progression
suggest?

Why should birth, usually a happy event, be presented in such an aura of unhappiness?

HE ALWAYS WANTED TO . . .

ANONYMOUS

He always wanted to explain things.
But no one cared.
So he drew.
Sometimes he would draw and it wasn't anything.
He wanted to carve it in stone or write it in the sky.   5
He would lie out on the grass and look up in the sky.
And it would be only him and the sky and the things
    inside him that needed saying.
And it was after that he drew the picture.
He kept it under his pillow and would let no one see it.   10
And he would look at it every night and think about it.
And when it was dark, and his eyes were closed, he could still see it.
And it was all of him.
And he loved it.
When he started school he brought it with him.   15
Not to show anyone, but just to have with him like a friend.
It was funny about school.
He sat in a square, brown desk
Like all the other square, brown desks
And he thought it should be red.   20
And his room was a square brown room.
Like all the other rooms.
And it was tight and close.
And stiff,
He hated to hold the pencil and chalk,   25
With his arm stiff and his feet flat on the floor,
Stiff,
With the teacher watching and watching.
The teacher came and spoke to him.
She told him to wear a tie like all the other boys.   30
He said he didn't like them.
And she said it didn't matter!
After that they drew.
And he drew all yellow and it was the way he felt about morning.
And it was beautiful.   35
The teacher came and smiled at him.
"What's this?" she said. "Why don't you draw something
    like Ken's drawing? Isn't that beautiful?"

After that his mother bought him a tie.
And he always drew airplanes and rocket ships like everyone else.
And he threw the old picture away.   40
And when he lay alone looking at the sky,
It was big and blue and all of everything,
But he wasn't anymore.
He was square inside
And brown,   45
And his hands were stiff.
And he was like everyone else.
And the things inside him that needed saying didn't need it anymore.
It had stopped pushing.
It was crushed.   50
Stiff,
Like everything else.

This poem may suggest the reasons behind the unhappy tone of "Infant Sorrow." What are they?

What does the poem say about today's youth?

The poem was given to a teacher in Regina, Saskatchewan, Canada by a twelfth grade student. Although we do not know if he wrote the poem, we do know that he committed suicide a few weeks later.

WHEN SOMETIMES

MARY LOU DENMAN

When sometimes the world does leave us, and our senses, freely spinning, put us to a most perplexing frame of mind, we are undone.

Then the vacuum and the pressure of the lightly dark noncolors seem so cooly warm surrounding, and the panic rends us dumb.

Out of order! Out of order! You are talking out of order! Please   5
forgive me; I need help now; I just don't know what to do.

For it happens only rarely, and I never build defenses, for I feel so surely certain when it leaves it won't return.

Yet it comes again: Sensation piercing cranial peace and order: never bedlam, yet an altered sense of being. Need for rest.   10

Need for warmth and for affection—sooner still for lack of worries: worries, bothers, troubles skirting through my mind and me afflicting.

Now I'm silent, pensive, frightened, never knowing when will finish this affliction. World console me! Now I'm hiding from myself.   15

I'll be better. Oh, don't worry. For the world will soon return,
but even while it's gone, I'll manage. Thanks for listening to me talk.

What mood is expressed here?
"Cooly warm" is an *oxymoron* (a paradox). Do you find any other oxymorons in the poem? How well do they suggest the feeling expressed? Why?

ON AN ECDYSIAST

JOHN CIARDI

She stripped herself of all except pretense.
By nature she and Nature lived to feud
over two words. Her life explains their sense:
born naked into the world, she left it nude.

How does the *denotation* (literal meaning) of *ecdysiast* help you understand the poem? What does the word suggest beyond its literal meaning?
Nature is used in two senses here. What are they?
What can be inferred from the words *naked* and *nude*?

ALBATROSS

JUDY COLLINS

The lady comes to the gate
Dressed in lavender and leather
Looking North to the sea
She finds the weather fine
She hears the steeple bells   5
Ringing through the orchard all the way from town
She watches seagulls fly
Silver on the ocean
Stitching through the waves the edges of the sky
Many people wander up the hills from all around you   10

Making up your memories and thinking they have found you
They cover you with veils of wonder
As if you were a bride
Young men holding violets are curious to know
If you have cried   15
And tell you why and ask you why
Any way you answer
Lace around the collars
Of the blouses of the ladies
Flowers from a Spanish friend   20
Of the family
The embroidery of your life
Holds you in and keeps you out
But you survive
Imprisoned in your bones   25
Behind the isinglass windows of your eyes.
And in the night the iron wheels
     rolling through the rain
Down the hills through the long grass
     to the sea,   30
And in the dark the hard bells
     ringing with pain
Come away alone.

Even now by the gate
With your long hair blowing,   35
And the colors of the day
That lie along your arms,
You must barter your life
To make sure you are living,
And the crowd that has come,   40
You give them the colors,
And the bells and the wind and the dreams.
Will there never be a prince who rides
Who rides along the sea and the mountains,
Scattering the sand and foam   45
Into amethyst fountains,
Riding up the hills from the beach
In the long summer grass,
Holding the sun in his hands
And shattering the isinglass?   50
Day and night and day again,
And people come and go away forever,
While the shining summer sea
Dances in the glass of your mirror,
While you search the waves for love   55

And your visions for a sign,
The knot of tears around your throat
Is crystalizing into your design.
And in the night the iron wheels
    rolling through the rain   60
Down the hills through the long grass
    to the sea,
And in the dark the hard bells
    ringing with pain,
Come away alone   65
Come away alone . . . with me.

In what sense is this lyric about an albatross?
What does the title suggest in relation to the subject of the lyric?
What kind of "lady" is described? Who is the "you" of the lyric?
Several *images* (mental pictures) are evoked here. What are they? How do they add to the subject?

PAST MIDNIGHT

EVGENIJ VINOKUROV

(Translated by Vytas Dukas)

Past midnight, simply
Break the pencil, crumble it
And write a forceful
        song
That dashes forth!   5
So that in the morning, before the dawn,
Before the East lights up,
It flies through the universe,
As a loose leaf from a notebook.
So that in the blue countries far away   10
It collapses in an avalanche,
With all the strength of burst lungs
In a song-leader with rosy cheeks,
Then, when you walk away from the table
To the window in the morning,   15
The song should come back to you
With the lips of singing streets.

The preceding poems dealt primarily with man's search for self-identity. This poem and the two that follow suggest man's need for recognition by others. Relate them to one another, showing the similarities and differences in ideas and manner of expression.

ODE TO THE WEST WIND

PERCY BYSSHE SHELLEY

I

O wild West Wind, thou breath of autumn's being,
Thou, from whose unseen presence the leaves dead
Are driven, like ghosts from an enchanter fleeing,

Yellow, and black, and pale, and hectic red,
Pestilence-stricken multitudes: O thou,　　　　　　　　　5
Who chariotest to their dark wintry bed

The wingèd seeds, where they lie cold and low,
Each like a corpse within its grave, until
Thine azure sister of the spring shall blow

Her clarion o'er the dreaming earth, and fill　　　　　　10
(Driving sweet buds like flocks to feed in air)
With living hues and odors plain and hill:

Wild Spirit, which art moving everywhere;
Destroyer and preserver; hear, oh, hear!

II

Thou on whose stream, mid the steep sky's commotion,　　15
Loose clouds like earth's decaying leaves are shed,
Shook from the tangled boughs of heaven and ocean,

Angels of rain and lightning: there are spread
On the blue surface of thine aery surge,
Like the bright hair uplifted from the head　　　　　　　20

Of some fierce Maenad, even from the dim verge
Of the horizon to the zenith's height,
The locks of the approaching storm. Thou dirge

Of the dying year, to which this closing night
Will be the dome of a vast sepulchre,   25
Vaulted with all thy congregated might

Of vapors, from whose solid atmosphere
Black rain, and fire, and hail will burst: oh, hear!

III

Thou who didst waken from his summer dreams
The blue Mediterranean, where he lay,   30
Lulled by the coil of his crystalline streams,

Beside a pumice isle in Baiae's bay,
And saw in sleep old palaces and towers
Quivering within the wave's intenser day,

All overgrown with azure moss and flowers   35
So sweet, the sense faints picturing them! Thou
For whose path the Atlantic's level powers

Cleave themselves into chasms, while far below
The sea-blooms and the oozy woods which wear
The sapless foliage of the ocean, know   40

Thy voice, and suddenly grow gray with fear,
And tremble and despoil themselves: oh hear!

IV

If I were a dead leaf thou mightest bear;
If I were a swift cloud to fly with thee;
A wave to pant beneath thy power, and share   45

The impulses of thy strength, only less free
Than thou, O uncontrollable! If even
I were as in my boyhood, and could be

The comrade of thy wanderings over heaven,
As then, when to outstrip thy skiey speed   50
Scarce seemed a vision; I would ne'er have striven

As thus with thee in prayer in my sore need,
Oh, lift me as a wave, a leaf, a cloud!
I fall upon the thorns of life! I bleed!

13

A heavy weight of hours has chained and bowed   55
One too like thee: tameless, and swift, and proud.

V

Make me thy lyre, even as the forest is:
What if my leaves are falling like its own!
The tumult of thy mighty harmonies

Will take from both a deep, autumnal tone,   60
Sweet though in sadness. Be thou, Spirit fierce,
My spirit! Be thou me, impetuous one!

Drive my dead thoughts over the universe
Like withered leaves to quicken a new birth!
And, by the incantation of this verse,   65

Scatter, as from an unextinguished hearth
Ashes and sparks, my words among mankind!
Be through my lips to unawakened earth

The trumpet of a prophecy! O, Wind,
If winter comes, can spring be far behind?   70

MY GOBLET

BLAIR H. ALLEN

Each bright piece
Each careful shape
Each special color
Like rainbow hues
In mosaic pattern
Forms my goblet
Of fragile
Glass
I worked
So hard   10
To create
So perfect
That
Shatters
So easily   15
When critics touch it

MY LAST DUCHESS

Ferrara

ROBERT BROWNING

That's my last Duchess painted on the wall,
Looking as if she were alive. I call
That piece a wonder, now: Frà Pandolf's hands
Worked busily a day, and there she stands.
Will't please you sit and look at her? I said   5
"Frà Pandolf" by design, for never read
Strangers like you that pictured countenance,
But to myself they turned (since none puts by
The curtain I have drawn for you, but I)
And seemed as they would ask me, if they durst,   10
How such a glance came there; so, not the first
Are you to turn and ask thus. Sir, 'twas not
Her husband's presence only, called that spot
Of joy into the Duchess' cheek: perhaps
Frà Pandolf chanced to say "Her mantle laps   15
Over my lady's wrist too much," or "Paint
Must never hope to reproduce the faint
Half-flush that dies along her throat": such stuff
Was courtesy, she thought, and cause enough
For calling up that spot of joy. She had   20
A heart—how shall I say?—too soon made glad,
Too easily impressed; she liked whate'er
She looked on, and her looks went everywhere.
Sir, 'twas all one! My favor at her breast,
The dropping of the daylight in the West,   25
The bough of cherries some officious fool
Broke in the orchard for her, the white mule
She rode with round the terrace—all and each
Would draw from her alike the approving speech,
Or blush, at least. She thanked men—good! but thanked   30
Somehow—I know not how—as if she ranked
My gift of a nine-hundred-years-old name
With anybody's gift. Who'd stoop to blame
This sort of trifling? Even had you skill
In speech—(which I have not)—to make your will   35
Quite clear to such an one, and say, "Just this
Or that in you disgusts me; here you miss,
Or there exceed the mark"—and if she let
Herself be lessoned so, nor plainly set
Her wits to yours, forsooth, and made excuse   40

15

—E'en then would be some stooping; and I choose
Never to stoop. Oh sir, she smiled, no doubt,
Whene'er I passed her; but who passed without
Much the same smile? This grew; I gave commands;
Then all smiles stopped together. There she stands   45
As if alive. Will't please you rise? We'll meet
The company below, then. I repeat,
The Count your master's known munificence
Is ample warrant that no just pretense
Of mine for dowry will be disallowed;   50
Though his fair daughter's self, as I avowed
At starting, is my object. Nay, we'll go
Together down, sir. Notice Neptune, though,
Taming a sea horse, thought a rarity,
Which Claus of Innsbruck cast in bronze for me!   55

This poem is set in Ferrara, a city in Italy, during the Renaissance, probably the sixteenth century. The Duke of Ferrara negotiates with an envoy from the Count for his next bride, the Count's daughter. The poem takes the form of a *dramatic monologue* (a poem in which the central speaker unwittingly reveals more of his character than he intends while talking about someone else).

Characterize the Duke as fully as possible. Everything in the poem is seen through his eyes. How reliable a narrator is he? How do we know? What does this imply about his last Duchess? About his feelings toward his next Duchess?

Irony (a discrepancy between what is said and what is meant) plays an important part in this poem. What ironies do you detect?

THE LOVE SONG OF J. ALFRED PRUFROCK

T. S. ELIOT

S'io credesse che mia risposta fosse
A persona che mai tornasse al mondo,
Questa fiamma staria senza più scosse.
Ma perciòcche giammai di questo fondo
Non torno vivo alcun, s'i'odo il vero.
Senza tema d'infamia ti rispondo.

Let us go then, you and I,
When the evening is spread out against the sky

Like a patient etherised upon a table;
Let us go, through certain half-deserted streets,
The muttering retreats   5
Of restless nights in one-night cheap hotels
And sawdust restaurants with oyster-shells:
Streets that follow like a tedious argument
Of insidious intent
To lead you to an overwhelming question . . .   10
Oh, do not ask, "What is it?"
Let us go and make our visit.

    In the room the women come and go
Talking of Michelangelo.

    The yellow fog that rubs its back upon the window-panes,   15
The yellow smoke that rubs its muzzle on the window-panes
Licked its tongue into the corners of the evening,
Lingered upon the pools that stand in drains,
Let fall upon its back the soot that falls from chimneys,
Slipped by the terrace, made a sudden leap,   20
And seeing that it was a soft October night,
Curled once about the house, and fell asleep.

    And indeed there will be time
For the yellow smoke that slides along the street,,
Rubbing its back upon the window-panes;   25
There will be time, there will be time
To prepare a face to meet the faces that you meet;
There will be time to murder and create,
And time for all the works and days of hands
That lift and drop a question on your plate;   30
Time for you and time for me,
And time yet for a hundred indecisions,
And for a hundred visions and revisions,
Before the taking of a toast and tea.

    In the room the women come and go   35
Talking of Michelangelo.

    And indeed there will be time
To wonder, "Do I dare?" and, "Do I dare?"
Time to turn back and descend the stair,
With a bald spot in the middle of my hair—   40
[They will say: "How his hair is growing thin!"]
My morning coat, my collar mounting firmly to the chin,
My necktie rich and modest, but asserted by a simple pin—
[They will say: "But how his arms and legs are thin!"]

17

Do I dare   45
Disturb the universe?
In a minute there is time
For decisions and revisions which a minute will reverse.

    For I have known them all already, known them all:—
Have known the evenings, mornings, afternoons,   50
I have measured out my life with coffee spoons;
I know the voices dying with a dying fall
Beneath the music from a farther room.
    So how should I presume?

    And I have known the eyes already, known them all—   55
The eyes that fix you in a formulated phrase,
And when I am formulated, sprawling on a pin,
When I am pinned and wriggling on the wall,
Then how should I begin
To spit out all the butt-ends of my days and ways?   60
    And how should I presume?

    And I have known the arms already, known them all—
Arms that are braceleted and white and bare
[But in the lamplight, downed with light brown hair!]
Is it perfume from a dress   65
That makes me so digress?
Arms that lie along a table, or wrap about a shawl.
    And should I then presume?
    And how should I begin?

          . . .

Shall I say, I have gone at dusk through narrow streets   70
And watched the smoke that rises from the pipes
Of lonely men in shirt-sleeves, leaning out of windows? . . .

    I should have been a pair of ragged claws
Scuttling across the floors of silent seas.

          . . .

And the afternoon, the evening, sleeps so peacefully!   75
Smoothed by long fingers,
Asleep . . . tired . . . or it malingers,
Stretched on the floor, here beside you and me.
Should I, after tea and cakes and ices,
Have the strength to force the moment to its crisis?   80
But though I have wept and fasted, wept and prayed,

Though I have seen my head [grown slightly bald] brought in
    upon a platter,
I am no prophet—and here's no great matter;
I have seen the moment of my greatness flicker,
And I have seen the eternal Footman hold my coat, and snicker,   85
And in short, I was afraid.

    And would it have been worth it, after all,
After the cups, the marmalade, the tea,
Among the porcelain, among some talk of you and me,
Would it have been worth while,   90
To have bitten off the matter with a smile,
To have squeezed the universe into a ball
To roll it toward some overwhelming question,
To say: "I am Lazarus, come from the dead,
Come back to tell you all, I shall tell you all"—   95
If one, settling a pillow by her head,
    Should say: "That is not what I meant at all.
    That is not it, at all."

    And would it have been worth it, after all,
Would it have been worth while,   100
After the sunsets and the dooryards and the sprinkled streets,
After the novels, after the teacups, after the skirts that
    trail along the floor—
And this, and so much more?—
It is impossible to say just what I mean!
But as if a magic lantern threw the nerves in patterns on   105
    a screen:
Would it have been worth while
If one, stealing a pillow or throwing off a shawl,
And turning toward the window, should say:
    "That is not it at all,
    That is not what I meant, at all."   110

    .   .   .

No! I am not Prince Hamlet, nor was meant to be;
Am an attendant lord, one that will do
To swell a progress, start a scene or two,
Advise the prince; no doubt, an easy tool,
Deferential, glad to be of use,   115
Politic, cautious, and meticulous;
Full of high sentence, but a bit obtuse;
At times, indeed, almost ridiculous—
Almost, at times, the Fool.

I grow old . . . I grow old . . .   120
I shall wear the bottoms of my trousers rolled.

Shall I part my hair behind? Do I dare to eat a peach?
I shall wear white flannel trousers, and walk upon the beach.
I have heard the mermaids singing, each to each.

I do not think that they will sing to me.   125

I have seen them riding seaward on the waves
Combing the white hair of the waves blown back
When the wind blows the water white and black.

We have lingered in the chambers of the sea
By sea-girls wreathed with seaweed red and brown   130
Till human voices wake us, and we drown.

This poem, like "My Last Duchess," is a dramatic monologue. Unlike Browning, however, Eliot uses *stream-of-consciousness* (representation of the workings of the mind). Prufrock is not speaking to us or to someone within the poem, like Browning's Duke; instead, he is thinking. The poem consists of the random thoughts that flit through his mind, and for this reason it may be more difficult to understand than Browning's poem.

You may also find this poem difficult because many *allusions* (references to things outside the poem) are made with which you may be unfamiliar. The prologue, for instance, quoted from Dante's *Inferno,* consists of lines spoken by one of the sinners in the Inferno. The sinner explains to Dante that he will relate his story to Dante only because he knows that Dante can never return to the world to tell the story to others. With your instructor's help, identify as many allusions as you can in the poem.

Whether or not you can identify many allusions, you should still be able to glean a fairly accurate picture of Prufrock. What does he look like? What kind of man is he? How does the poem tell you that?

Where is Prufrock going? Why? Will he achieve his goal? How do you know?

Who are the "you" and "I" of the first line?

What ironies does the poem suggest?

What does Prufrock's predicament imply about modern man? How does this implication coincide with your experience?

MISCONCEPTION

BONNIE BUCHANAN

He was a
freak.
It was obvious.
His face was an
oddity.   5
His body;
a spectacle.
He held out his deformed
thumb to cars full
of conveniently   10
blind people;
who had to rush home
to deceiving mirrors
and thank the Fates
for fashionable faces.   15
Magnificent minds
aren't being worn
this year.

Could it be
he wanted   20
more than just a
ride?

UNTITLED

MICHAEL POGLIANO

old smell carpets
catch bits of cracking walls
among flap-up window shades

humid south-side air
presses heavy   5
over my watching
with a loud sign
blinking
VACANCY
in my brain   10

here i'm tired
holding a thousand cups of coffee
& walking a hundred years
across the room

speak to me!   15
—the only voice
a toilet flushing overhead

The speaker in this poem is much like the hitchhiker in "Misconception," but the respective tones and themes of the two poems differ greatly. Compare and contrast them. What specific things in the poems contribute to these differences?

ELEANOR RIGBY

JOHN LENNON and *PAUL McCARTNEY*

Ah, look at all the lonely people!
Ah, look at all the lonely people!

Eleanor Rigby picks up the rice in the church
Where a wedding has been.
Lives in a dream.   5
Waits at the window, wearing the face that she
   keeps in a jar by the door.
Who is it for?

All the lonely people, where do they all come from?
All the lonely people, where do they all belong?

Father McKenzie writing the words of a sermon   10
   that no one will hear—
No one comes near. Look at him working, darning his
   socks in the night when there's nobody there.
What does he care?

All the lonely people, where do they all come from?
All the lonely people, where do they all belong?

Eleanor Rigby, died in the church and was buried   15
   along with her name, nobody came.

Father McKenzie, wiping the dirt from his hands as
   he walks from the grave.
No one was saved.

All the lonely people, where do they all come from?
All the lonely people, where do they all belong?

Who is Eleanor Rigby? Why does she keep her face in a jar by the
door?
Who are all the lonely people?
Why doesn't anyone hear Father McKenzie's sermon? Why is no one
saved?
How do *images* (mental pictures) contribute to the total lyric?
The lyric poses several questions. Are they answered? What does this
suggest?

THE BIG I

JOHN HALL WHEELOCK

A bird with a big eye
In at my open window poked his head,
And fixed me with a big eye.
"Who are you? What do you want?" I said.
"Me? You mean you don't know me?" he made reply,   5
"Why, I am I. Who are you?"
"I, too, am I," I bashfully admitted.
Now here was a big I-dea to work upon,
For if each one is I, must we not all be one?
Then I am one in all, and all are one in me.   10
I observed, thinking it over carefully,
That I wondered, this being true,
What made us feel so separate, so alone.
"*I* did," shouted the bird,
And I turned to strangle him, but he was flown.   15

What is the relationship between the "I's"?
Why does the bird have a "big eye"?
What is the meaning of line fourteen?
What can we infer from the poem about man and his relationship
both to himself and to others?

FOR A FRIEND

ROBERT CREELEY

Who remembers him also, he thinks
(but to himself and as himself).

Himself alone is dominant
in a world of no one else.

FASCINATION

PAT FOLK

My presence seemed to force the air to stir
In unfelt whirlwinds twirling everywhere.
A swirl of brilliance dangled in my sight
And flared my gaze on lines quick thrown and reeled.
Such incandescent threads of splendid glow   5
Those many-fingered tentacles of lure.
Those syncopated gleams hurled stars to birth
And blasted golden, crystal air to worlds.
A moment, no, a fraction less it blazed
Then drifted low and lost the sun and me.   10
It left no stain. Its life-shine was its mark.
Complete and innocent beauty was its height.
It was a fleck, a speck of dust that's all,
Responding to my breathing and the light.

What is the poem's *controlling image* (the image around which the
entire poem is built)? What mood does this image create? How does this
mood relate to theme?

TO A MAD FRIEND

PETER DAVISON

I may look fine at the moment, but like you
I have capered and somersaulted in the street,
While, hoisted upon my shoulders, someone's face
Smiled at my friends and answered the telephone;

Or hovered, like a fish with nose against   5
A rock, in elements I could not breathe.
You've seen us in every land you've travelled through:
Our ties were tied, our shoes were always shined,
But icy eyes and tightness around the smile
Are marks enough to know your brothers by.   10
Rest easier, friend: we've all walked through your dreams
And are no strangers to that company.

Who is the "us" of the poem?
Whose dreams are walked through? To whom is the speaker talking?
What are the implications of what he is saying?

THESE LIVES

HARVEY SHAPIRO

When everything is prepared for the feast—
August high-vaulted,
The clouds a classic scroll—

The painter must have a hypo.
What's the meaning of his crying jag?   5
The wife calls the doctor.

The dolphin floats gently to shore
On the winds of his own corruption.
Even the gulls respect that stench.

What happens to these lives?   10

A strange mixture of feast, clouds, painter, hypo, dolphin, winds, and
gulls exists here. How are they all related?

EREHWON

ELIOT GLASSHEIM

My heart is homeless in the driving bus
Across the desert, east to west,
Past swollen cactus lurking off the road

And flat grey land made murky by the moon.
My heart is homeless, caught between;   5
A life at either end, dots on the map,
Myself stretched taut along the road.
I carry on my back a shell I once called home.

This poem may remind you of the long trip between college and
home. What does the setting contribute to the total poem?
What is the speaker saying?
What is the "shell" he carries on his back? Why does he no longer call
it home?
Comment on the significance of the title. That it was originally a title
for a utopian novel may suggest certain things to you.

TO SMITH

BARBARA MILES

all I know is this
if you are Smith
then I am Smith
and all my words
are Smith's own words   5

if you are Smith
the sun is Smith
and stars are all
the little Smith kids

one grand Smith is It   10
life
if you are Smith

I've seen the best minds
of my generation
going   15
stark raving Smith

if Smith we are
Smith we must be
and Smith into
eternity   20

sexy old Sigmund Smith
Smitty Einstein
Marlon Smith and
Smithwig von Beethoven

Jazz Smith Wm   25
Shakesmith, the pith
of Smith
Michelangelo Buonarroti
Smith
if this is Smith   30

it's all Smith
Smith is god to Smith
and God is Smith
with Smith inside

Who is Smith?
Relate this poem to "The Big I." Relate it to John Donne's statement
made in 1623: "No man is an island, entire of itself; every man is a piece
of the continent, a part of the main. . . ."

WALKING

BETSY RICHARDS

I was walking one day
On the flat of a razor blade
Tracing out the little
Writing patterns, watching
For the center pit.   5
Then I looked up and saw
Space, free and high.
The razor lurched
Suddenly I was ankle-deep in pain
Seeing beauty, light, and other abstract things   10
Balancing on a sweet thin line of pain.
The razor lurched again.
I'm back to little patterns
Except for my scars maybe it was just a dream.
But I'll go on with it . . .   15
Maybe the razor will lurch again.

What does the razor blade suggest?
What is the implied connection between pain and beauty?
Why does the speaker seem to desire the inevitable pain of the razor,
should it lurch again? What does that desire imply?

MIRROR, MIRROR

BONNIE BUCHANAN

Sometimes,
the world gets too big
for us to handle, and
we drop it on our toes.
We're so busy   5
trying to keep pace
with the BIG society
that we forget about
the little things;
like chasing squittels   10
and
firesides.
We become so involved
in all-out efforts
to "find ourselves,"   15
when,
all it takes
is an objective glance
in the mirror
and   20
a friend standing by
with smelling salts.

What is the BIG society? What does it imply?
Although you won't find *squittel* in the dictionary, define it in your
own words.
What is the poet saying?

THE TREEHOUSE

JAMES EMANUEL

To every man
His treehouse,

A green splice in the humping years,
Spartan with narrow cot
And prickly door.   5

To every man
His twilight flash
Of luminous recall

    of tiptoe years
    in leaf-stung flight;   10
    of days of squirm and bite
    that waved antennas through the grass;
    of nights
    when every moving thing
    was girlshaped,   15
    expectantly turning.

To every man
His house below
And his house above—
With perilous stairs   20
Between.

A *dichotomy* (separation) is maintained between up and down; however, it changes by the end of the poem. How? What is the progression?

What is meant by "humping years"; "twilight flash"; "luminous recall"; "tiptoe years"; "leaf-stung flight"; "days of squirm and bite"?

2
Poetry
and Perception

Now that we have dipped briefly into a few poems, we are ready to delve into poetry in earnest. One tool that may be necessary for complete understanding of the poems is a good dictionary. We said before that a poem says the most in the fewest possible words. Every word is tremendously important. Not knowing the meaning of even a single word in a short poem may cloud the meaning of the entire poem. The following Beatle *lyric* (a poem that expresses the emotion or sentiment of the poet, rather than telling a story) is an example.

LUCY IN THE SKY WITH DIAMONDS

JOHN LENNON and PAUL McCARTNEY

Picture yourself in a boat on a river,
With tangerine trees and marmalade skies
Somebody calls you, you answer quite slowly,
A girl with kaleidoscope eyes.
Cellophane flowers of yellow and green,
Towering over your head.
Look for the girl with the sun in her eyes,
And she's gone.
Lucy in the sky with diamonds.
Follow her down to a bridge by a fountain
Where rocking horse people eat marshmallow pies,
Everyone smiles as you drift past the flowers,
That grow so incredibly high.

Newspaper taxis appear on the shore,
Waiting to take you away.
Climb in the back with your head in the clouds,
And you're gone.
Lucy in the sky with diamonds,
Picture yourself on a train in a station,
With plasticine porters with looking glass ties,
Suddenly someone is there at the turnstile,
The girl with the kaleidoscope eyes.

Although it may be extremely difficult because the Beatles' lyrics are often completely synchronized with the music, for the sake of this analysis let us divorce the words from the music and treat the lyric solely as a poem.

The title, a springboard into the poem itself, sometimes tells us explicitly what the poem is about. More often, however, it only hints. "Lucy in the Sky with Diamonds" *seems* to be fairly simple and forthright. There are three concretes: Lucy, a girl who plays a role in the poem; sky, ranging from blues and grays to black, floating above us and enveloping the earth; and diamonds, precious stones, usually clear, many-faceted, sparkling, highly coveted by girls, and often given as tokens of love. We have no difficulty imagining Lucy (any girl) with diamonds, then. But the title becomes more ambiguous when we consider the phrase "in the sky." Diamonds in the sky? Perhaps. Stars have often been compared with diamonds. But the title does not say exactly that; rather, it tells us that Lucy is in the sky. Could it be that Lucy, smothered in her diamond rings, is skimming high overhead by jet from place to place? Or could she be some sort of constellation twinkling in the sky? Perhaps both? Perhaps neither! We must proceed further into the poem to find out.

Taking a second step into the poem, we skim it quickly to isolate any unfamiliar words. Two possibile unknowns might be *kaleidoscope* and *plasticine*. A kaleidoscope, we may recall from childhood, is a tubelike toy in which we viewed changing designs made by bits of colored glass reflected in mirrors. We may also remember finding it impossible to share a particularly beautiful kaleidoscopic pattern with a friend. The minute we moved the tube—no matter how carefully—the design changed. We might turn to the dictionary at this point. There we find that not only is a kaleidoscope the toy we remember enjoying, but the word also denotes anything that changes constantly. From this, we can infer that the girl's eyes, like the kaleidoscope, constantly change.

Plasticine, a thing of the past now that "Play Dough" and "Silly Putty" are made, may force our return to the dictionary. There we find that plasticine, a puttylike substance made in various colors, is used by children for modeling clay, but, unlike clay or "Play Dough," plasticine never hardens. It remains pliable forever. In short, the shape of plasticine, like the design in the kaleidoscope, also changes readily. A *motif* (recurring pattern) of change begins to emerge from the words in the poem. Notice, however, that this motif emerges as much from the *connotation* (implied or associated meaning) of the words as it does from their *denotation* (literal or dictionary meaning). The poet, more than any other writer, uses words as much for their connotative as for their denotative value—something extremely important to keep in mind as we read.

Once we have explored the possibilities of title and of denotations and connotations of words, we can move on to the final and somewhat more complex step of reading the poem. Basically, this step involves giving the poem several careful readings aloud (poetry is meant to be heard, so the sound is often tremendously important), defining any problems arising in the poem, posing questions about them, and trying to resolve these questions. There are dozens of questions we could ask about almost any poem, but for the sake of simplicity let's divide them into four categories: (1) the speaker, (2) the central purpose, (3) the techniques of the poet, and (4) the skill of the poet. To clarify, let us examine each of these categories individually.

First of all, let's deal with the voice in the poem—the persona or speaker. *Who is he?* Rarely is he simply the author talking directly to the reader. Instead, he usually emerges as a kind of mask behind which the author hides his true identity and into whose mouth he places the words he wishes to convey to the reader. Sometimes this persona is explicitly or implicitly named in the poem; at others, he is an anonymous voice. Sometimes he is of the same sex and background as the poet; often he is neither. In "Lucy in the Sky" the speaker remains anonymous. A voice from the lyric asks us to take an imaginary trip ("Picture yourself in a boat on a river . . . "), but no words explicitly tell or implicitly suggest his identity.

Merely discovering the speaker's identity, however (if, indeed, we do), does not suffice. An even more important question to ask about the speaker may be "What kind of person is he?" Although we may be unable to determine this with any certainty in "Lucy," we can surmise from the speaker's vivid description that he has been through the same kind of experience that he asks his audience to picture.

Another question that may be important to our understanding of the poem is "To whom does the speaker speak?" At times he talks directly to the reader; at other times he talks to someone else who may or may not be in the poem. In "Lucy" the speaker talks directly to us, outside the poem, and asks us to imagine ourselves in a certain situation.

Two other questions about the speaker are "What occasion prompts him to speak?" and "Is the setting important in relation to the speaker or to what he says?" In "Lucy" the occasion seems to be relatively unimportant; it can be determined only very tentatively. But the setting is mentioned in great detail. It is probably in a city, as the fountain, taxis, and train station suggest. Whenever the speaker mentions setting, however, one thing stands out as unique: its complete unreality. The skies are not blue, grey, or black, the usual colors for a sky; they are "marmalade skies." The people differ from the usual hurried people found in most cities; they are "rocking horse people." The flowers are made of cellophane, the taxis of newspaper, the porters of plasticine, and their ties of mirrors. A strange kind of city, to say the least! All this suggests, of course, a removal or escape from reality. The setting, then, becomes significant in that it departs from the real world and places us in a surrealistic environment.

Once we have determined all the important aspects surrounding the speaker, our next problem is the poem's central purpose. *Every good poem has some kind of central purpose.* In other words, poems are more than a group of words thrown haphazardly together. On the contrary, the poet has a definite goal when he creates a poem. He may wish to tell a story, as Robert Graves does in the following poem.

CALL IT A GOOD MARRIAGE

ROBERT GRAVES

Call it a good marriage—
For no one ever questioned
Her warmth, his masculinity,
Their interlocking views;
Except one stray graphologist
Who frowned in speculation
At her h's and her s's,
His p's and w's.

Though few would still subscribe
To the monogamic axiom
That strife below the hip-bones
Need not estrange the heart,
Call it a good marriage:
More drew those two together,
Despite a lack of children,
Than pulled them apart.

Call it a good marriage:
They never fought in public,
They acted circumspectly
And faced the world with pride;
Thus the hazards of their love-bed
Were none of our damned business—
Till as jurymen we sat on
Two deaths by suicide.

Or perhaps the poet wishes to reveal some aspect of human character, as Peter Davison does in "Out of Tune":

OUT OF TUNE

PETER DAVISON

Irving, pleasant-spoken, liked by dogs,
Children, earns his neighbors' shining smiles,
The respect of spokesmen. Yet he stumbles,
Sees only glare in sun, drabness in the green
Of leaves, futility in the flight of a bird.
Winter sours his mouth with taste of iron.
Scent of love gives off smell of decay.
At the core of himself nothing can be heard
But thumping of blood. Thoughts are cold as slate.

Wrapped like a fly in the spiderweb of the world,
What would he give now to have flown
Sure as the man on skis whose swiftness leans
Against the snowy shoulder of the hill?

Even more simply, the poet may wish to convey the impression of a scene. Hart Crane paints a vivid word-picture of early spring:

MARCH

HART CRANE

Awake to the cold light
of wet wind running

twigs in tremors. Walls
are naked. Twilights raw—
and when the sun taps steeples
their glistenings dwindle
upward . . .

       March
slips along the ground
like a mouse under pussy
willows, a little hungry.
The vagrant ghost of winter,
is it this that keeps the chimney
busy still? For something still
nudges shingles and windows:

but waveringly,—this ghost,
this slate-eyed saintly wraith
of winter wanes
and knows its waning.

Then again, the poet may wish to convey a mood or an emotion. Shelley does that in "A Dirge":

A DIRGE

PERCY BYSSHE SHELLEY

Rough wind, that moanest loud
    Grief too sad for song;
Wild wind, when sullen cloud
    Knells all the night long;
Sad storm, whose tears are vain,
Bare woods, whose branches strain,
Deep caves and dreary main—
    Wail, for the world's wrong!

A poet may want to convey an idea or an attitude about something in his world. Using the *clichés* (trite or overworked phrases) often related to racial discrimination, the following speaker's attitude about the entire human race is clear:

DISCRIMINATION

KENNETH REXROTH

I don't mind the human race.
I've got pretty used to them
In these past twenty-five years.
I don't mind if they sit next
To me on streetcars, or eat
In the same restaurants, if
It's not at the same table.
However, I don't approve
Of a woman I respect
Dancing with one of them. I've
Tried asking them to my home
Without success. I shouldn't
Care to see my own sister
Marry one. Even if she
Loved him, think of the children.
Their art is interesting,
But certainly barbarous.
I'm sure, if given a chance,
They'd kill us all in our beds.
And you must admit, they smell.

Occasionally, a poem is written which seems to achieve all these central purposes at one time. Such a poem is Robert Frost's "Out, Out—."

"OUT, OUT—"

ROBERT FROST

The buzz saw snarled and rattled in the yard
And made dust and dropped stove-length sticks of wood,
Sweet-scented stuff when the breeze drew across it.
And from there those that lifted eyes could count
Five mountain ranges one behind the other
Under the sunset far into Vermont.
And the saw snarled and rattled, snarled and rattled,
As it ran light, or had to bear a load.
And nothing happened: day was all but done.
Call it a day, I wish they might have said
To please the boy by giving him the half hour

That a boy counts so much when saved from work.
His sister stood beside them in her apron
To tell them "Supper." At the word, the saw,
As if to prove saws knew what supper meant,
Leaped out at the boy's hand, or seemed to leap—
He must have given the hand. However it was,
Neither refused the meeting. But the hand!
The boy's first outcry was a rueful laugh,
As he swung toward them holding up the hand,
Half in appeal, but half as if to keep
The life from spilling. Then the boy saw all—
Since he was old enough to know, big boy
Doing a man's work, though a child at heart—
He saw all spoiled. "Don't let him cut my hand off—
The doctor, when he comes. Don't let him, sister!"
So. But the hand was gone already.
The doctor put him in the dark of ether.
He lay and puffed his lips out with his breath.
And then—the watcher at his pulse took fright.
No one believed. They listened at his heart.
Little—less—nothing!—and that ended it.
No more to build on there. And they, since they
Were not the one dead, turned to their affairs.

Not only has Frost managed to create a mood and paint a scene, but he also tells a story, reveals an aspect of human character, and expresses an attitude—a real feat in so short a poem! So skillfully has he accomplished each of these that the poem seems to have several simultaneous central purposes, any one of which might be discussed as *the* central purpose.

However, we can paraphrase the central purpose of many poems in a single sentence. We could probably paraphrase the central purpose of "Lucy in the Sky with Diamonds" something like this: "The central purpose of this poem appears to be to impart an impression of a scene." (Because many poems are open to multiple interpretation, such tentative words as *appear* and *seem* are handy when discussing poetry.) The scene, as we noted earlier, is a strange mixture of the real and the unreal—the focus wavering constantly between one and the other. In fact, one student's interpretation of the lyric seems to be valid: "The poem tells what it is like to take a trip on LSD." The same student pointed to what he considered important evidence for his interpretation in the title of the song: "*Lucy ... Sky ... Diamonds.*" He might also have pointed to the various modes of transportation (boat, taxi, train), the surrealistic landscape (cellophane flowers of enormous size, marmalade skies, rocking horse people, newspaper taxis, and plasticine porters), the dilating eyes of the girl (kaleidoscope eyes), and, if he wished to deal with the total song, to the eerie quality of the music in the second half of the song. The Beatles effectively exploit all these things, and all of them contribute to the strange effect of the song on its audience and lend credence to the interpretation that the lyric is indeed about "tripping out" on drugs.

We should note that everything we deduced about "Lucy" (interpreting a poem *is* something like sleuthing a mystery) came from internal evidence in the poem. And we should emphasize that no matter how much we know about the poet, no matter how interesting his life may be, all the information necessary to interpret a poem can usually be found within the poem itself. It makes little difference whether the poet is male or female, black or white, soldier or pacifist; the persona he creates, the things that persona says, and how he says them within the poem are what is important.

We have almost conquered the interpretation of the poem; what is left is to determine *how* the poet achieved his central purpose (which we have already done to some extent in arriving at the central purpose) and *how well* he achieved it (which involves evaluation). We will discuss each poetic technique in detail later in the book; here we will simply list a few for reference: diction, imagery, figurative language, allusion, meter, rhythm, and sound patterns. All appear to some extent in most poems, but one or more usually predominate over the others in individual poems. "Lucy in the Sky with Diamonds," for example, depends primarily on *diction* (word choice) and *imagery* (pictures evoked in the reader's imagination by diction)—distortion being the keyword—for its effect. If we had not divorced the lyric from its music, however, we would certainly have had to mention surrealistic sound patterns as being at least as important as surrealistic images.

Finally, we ask the question "How well has the poet achieved his purpose?" Novice poetry students may feel fairly helpless at this point. But anyone who reads with understanding can qualify as a critic. Assuming that we have followed the steps in the previous discussion meticulously, we have probably read with a fair degree of understanding. Our critical judgment, then, if based on and supported by the text of the poem, is just as valid as anyone else's. We need only check over the following list to reach our final critical conclusions:

I. What does the title tell us about the poem?
II. What do the words mean? Denotative meaning? Connotative meaning?
III. What problems does the poem present?
    A. Who is the speaker?
        1. What kind of person is he?

2. To whom is he speaking?
3. What is the occasion? Is it important to the poem?
4. What is the setting? Is it important to the poem?

B. What is the central purpose of the poem? Paraphrase it in one sentence. Does the poem do one (or more) of these things:
   1. Tell a story?
   2. Reveal character?
   3. Impart the vivid impression of a scene?
   4. Express a mood or emotion?
   5. Convey an idea or attitude?

C. How is the central purpose achieved? What technique (or combination of techniques) does the poet use?
   1. Diction? (See Chapter 4, "Poetry, Subject; and Diction.")
   2. Imagery? (See Chapter 6, "Poetry and Image.")
   3. Figurative language? (See Chapter 6.)
   4. Allusion? (See Chapter 6.)
   5. Meter and rhythm? (See Chapter 8, "Poetry and Cadence.")
   6. Sound patterns? (See Chapter 10, "Poetry and Melody.")

D. How well is the central purpose achieved? Base your evaluation on all the preceding criteria.

AFTERTHOUGHTS

1. Listen closely to the Beatles' rendition of George Harrison's "While My Guitar Gently Weeps." (Lyrics are on page 97 of this book.) Discuss the relationship between words and music.
2. Analyze how the poet achieves his central purpose in each of the following poems: "Call it a Good Marriage," "Out of Tune," "March," "A Dirge," "Discrimination," and "Out, Out—."

3
Man and
the Other Sex

Woman? Oh, woman is a consummate rage,
but dead, or asleep, she pleases.
Take her. She has two excellent seasons.

EZRA POUND

   Throughout the history of literature—and, indeed, of human
thought itself—few topics have so fascinated man as the relationship
between the sexes. Woman, only recently considered as other than chattel
to her man, has eternally mystified him on the one hand and exasperated
him on the other. As a result, throughout the ages he has attempted to
capture his ambivalent feelings and to explain this many-faceted, latter-
day Eve in song, fiction, drama, and poetry. Ancient Norse Eddas sang
of a chameleon-like woman who was slave, helpmate, temptress, and bold
warrior. Greeks created deities of love and peace in the shape of woman
and then built temples to her. Biblical woman of the Old and New
Testaments was extremely complex: she could be from the most evil to the
most pure of beings. Medieval troubadours placed woman on a pedestal,
to be worshiped in a precise, courtly fashion. Victorians pulled her down
again and viewed her as a mere "lesser man." Even today, in an age of
far-reaching scientific and sociological advances, woman continues to
mystify and exasperate man as much as ever.
   Represented here are all the ambivalent attitudes about the other sex
and her relationship to man; interestingly, most of the thoughts about
woman found here and elsewhere were written by mystified men. Only

40

recently has woman broken her long silence and begun to speak out about herself and *her* relationship to the opposite sex. Feminine viewpoints are represented here by Barbara Miles's poems and by Anne Spencer's "Letter to my Sister." From the masculine point of view, however, we find woman represented as vindictive ("Barbara Allan"), scheming (Milton's "Eve"), lust provoking (the *carpe diem* poems), shallow (Eliot's secretary), and cruel (Meredith's wife). These are but a few of the ways man tends to see woman; none of them really understand or explain her.

CAST UP

LAWRENCE FERLINGHETTI

Cast up
      the heart flops over
            gasping 'Love'

    a foolish fish which tries to draw
      its breath from flesh of air   5

And no one there to hear its death
        among the sad bushes
    where the world rushes by
        in a blather of asphalt and delay

What is the effect of the phrase "flesh of air"?
What is "a blather of asphalt and delay"?

BAD DOG

BARBARA MILES

    lust
    is a lonely
    lost
    lewd sack
    of flesh   5
    creeping around
    the lowdown

parts
of town
like a sad dog   10
with
hungry tail
between its legs
looking
for a lovebone   15
to get
hung up on

love
fill up my belly
love   20
lick my face
and
I'll lick yours
love
make ugly   25
beautiful
love
don't treat me
like a dog

RAVAGED

GRETCHEN CRAFTS

LOVE kicked down the door of existence
and, with one swipe of her cruel hand,
dashed contentment to bits!

PEACE RAVAGED,
Caution, shattered, tinkled to earth   5
and was ground to dust.
Serenity gasped, clutched wildly at the brink,
and tumbled into the abyss,
spiraling slowly downward,
like a hawk pierced by an arrow.   10

REASON mouldered in a corner.
Cobwebs gripped the mind.
Caught in the vortex,
REALITY WAS DEAD!

"Ravaged" and "bad dog" present two more ideas about love. Compare and contrast them with "Cast Up." How do these concepts of love relate to your ideas and experience?

THE PENNYCANDYSTORE BEYOND THE EL

LAWRENCE FERLINGHETTI

<pre>
The pennycandystore beyond the El
is where I first
                fell in love
                        with unreality
Jellybeans glowed in the semi-gloom   5
of that september afternoon
A cat upon the counter moved among
                        the licorice sticks
                and tootsie rolls
        and Oh Boy Gum   10

Outside the leaves were falling as they died

A wind had blown away the sun

A girl ran in
Her hair was rainy
Her breasts were breathless in the little room   15

Outside the leaves were falling
                and they cried
                Too soon! too soon!
</pre>

What contrasting images are evoked? How do they relate to the theme and contribute to the total effect?
Why do the falling leaves cry "Too soon!"?

PAST TIME

HARVEY SHAPIRO

I believe we came together
Out of ignorance not love,
Both being shy and hunted in the city.

43

In the hot summer, touching each other,
Amazed at how love could come   5
Like a waterfall, with frightening force
And bruising sleep. Waking at noon,
Touching each other for direction,
Out of ignorance not love.

"Past Time" and "The Pennycandystore" are both about young love. Considering both ideas and diction, compare and contrast them. How do these two depictions of love differ from those immediately preceding them? How do they relate to your ideas about love?

THE MOMENT

THEODORE ROETHKE

We passed the ice of pain,
And came to a dark ravine,
And there we sang with the sea:
The wide, the bleak abyss
Shifted with our slow kiss.   5

Space struggled with time;
The gong of midnight struck
The naked absolute.
Sound, silence sang as one.

All flowed: without, within;   10
Body met body, we
Created what's to be.

What else to say?
We end in joy.

To what does the title refer?
Is there more than one possible interpretation to this poem?

44

Man and the Other Sex

INVASION

or

(TELEPATHY TO SOMEONE SPECIAL)

BLAIR H. ALLEN

My mind
All my power
All my concentration
All my deepest self
All the words she loves   5

THRUST
Into space

Hoping to invade
Her thoughts
Wherever   10
She may be

A sudden image
FLASHES

Like a ghost
Myself   15
Confronts her

She stiffens
Hand over her pounding heart

Wondering how

How does the diction of "Invasion" relate to the title?
What effect do the words *THRUST* and *FLASHES* have?

PICTURE OF A NUDE IN A MACHINE SHOP

WILLIAM CARLOS WILLIAMS

Picture of a Nude in a Machine Shop

and foundry,
        (that's art)
a red ostrich plume
in her hair: 5

Sweat and muddy water,
coiled fuse-strips
             surround her
poised sitting—
(between red, parted   10
           curtains)

the right leg
         (stockinged)
up!
    beside the point—   15
at ease.

Light as a glove, light
as her black gloves!
Modeled as a shoe, a woman's
high heeled shoe!   20
—the other leg stretched
out
    bare
        (toward the top—
and upward)
          as   25
the smeared hide under
shirt and pants
stiff with grease and dirt
is bare—
        approaching   30
the centrum

        (disguised)
the metal to be devalued!

      —bare as
a blow-torch flame,   35
        undisguised.

Comment on the contrasts in this poem.
The poem contains several ambiguities. What are they? Do they add
to or detract from the total poem? Why?
How does the image of woman here compare to that in "The Penny-
candystore"? What do the settings contribute to these images?

BARBARA ALLAN

ANONYMOUS

It was in and about the Martinmas time,
  When the green leaves were a-fallin',
That Sir John Graeme in the West Country
  Fell in love with Barbara Allan.

He sent his man down through the town   5
  To the place where she was dwellin':
"O haste and come to my master dear,
  Gin¹ ye be Barbara Allan."

O slowly, slowly rase² she up,
  To the place where he was lyin',   10
And when she drew the curtain by:
  "Young man, I think you're dyin'."

"O it's I'm sick, and very, very sick,
  And 'tis a' for Barbara Allan."
"O the better for me ye sal³ never be,   15
  Though your heart's blood were a-spillin'.

"O dinna ye mind,⁴ young man," said she,
  "When ye the cups were fillin',
That ye made the healths gae⁵ round and round,
  And slighted Barbara Allan?"   20

He turned his face unto the wall,
  And death with him was dealin':
"Adieu, adieu, my dear friends all,
  And be kind to Barbara Allan."

¹ if
² rose
³ shall
⁴ remember
⁵ go

And slowly, slowly, rase she up,   25
  And slowly, slowly left him;
And sighing said she could not stay,
  Since death of life had reft[6] him.

She had not gane[7] a mile but twa,[8]
  When she heard the dead-bell knellin',   30
And every jow[9] that the dead-bell ga'ed[10]
  It cried, "Woe to Barbara Allan!"

"O mother, mother, make my bed,
  O make it soft and narrow:
Since my love died for me today,   35
  I'll die for him tomorrow."

The ballad is one of the chief links between ancient and modern literature. This is only one of many versions of an old English ballad. Notice its form. What is peculiar about it?

A ballad usually tells a tragic story. What happens in "Barbara Allan"?

THE FALL

from *Paradise Lost*

JOHN MILTON

So saying, her rash hand in evil hour,
Forth reaching to the fruit, she plucked, she eat.
Earth felt the wound, and Nature from her seat
Sighing through all her works gave signs of woe,
That all was lost. Back to the thicket slunk   5
The guilty serpent, and well might, for Eve
Intent now wholly on her taste, naught else
Regarded; such delight till then, as seemed,
In fruit she never tasted, whether true
Or fancied so, through expectation high   10
Of knowledge; nor was godhead from her thought.

[6] deprived
[7] gone
[8] two
[9] stroke
[10] made

Greedily she engorged without restraint,
And knew not eating death: satiate at length,
And heightened as with wine, jocund and boon,
Thus to herself she pleasingly began: 15
"O sovereign, virtuous, precious of all trees
In Paradise! of operation blest
To sapience, hitherto obscured, infamed,
And thy fair fruit let hang, as to no end
Created; but henceforth my early care,   20
Not without song each morning, and due praise
Shall tend thee, and the fertile burden ease
Of thy full branches offered free to all;
Till dieted by thee I grow mature
In knowledge, as the gods who all things know;   25
Though others envy what they cannot give:
For had the gift been theirs, it had not here
Thus grown. Experience, next to thee I owe,
Best guide; not following thee I had remained
In ignorance; thou open'st Wisdom's way,   30
And giv'st access, though secret she retire.
And I perhaps am secret; Heaven is high,
High and remote to see from thence distinct
Each thing on Earth; and other care perhaps
May have diverted from continual watch   35
Our great Forbidder, safe with all his spies
About him. But to Adam in what sort
Shall I appear? Shall I to him make known
As yet my change, and give him to partake
Full happiness with me, or rather not,   40
But keep the odds of knowledge in my power
Without copartner? so to add what wants
In female sex, the more to draw his love,
And render me more equal, and perhaps,
A thing not undesirable, sometime   45
Superior: for, inferior, who is free?
This may be well: but what if God have seen
And death ensue? Then I shall be no more,
And Adam, wedded to another Eve,
Shall live with her enjoying, I extinct;   50
A death to think. Confirmed then I resolve,
Adam shall share with me in bliss or woe:
So dear I love him, that with him all deaths
I could endure, without him live no life."

This episode from *Paradise Lost* takes place in the Garden of Eden immediately after Satan, in the form of a beguiling serpent, has con-

vinced Eve that she should taste the forbidden fruit. He uses her vanity
to promote her act, telling her she will become godlike if she eats. Sum-
marize briefly, mentioning specific lines, what happens in the poem.
Why does Nature give signs of woe? What does this suggest?
What happens to Eve when she tastes the fruit? Why does she worship
the tree? What are the implications of this act?
What does Eve debate about in the final third of the poem? What is
her final decision? Why?
Compare Milton's account of Eve's act to the account in the Old
Testament. How has Milton changed the story? What effect do these
changes have on the reader?

TO HIS COY MISTRESS

ANDREW MARVELL

Had we but world enough, and time,
This coyness, lady, were no crime.
We would sit down, and think which way
To walk, and pass our long love's day.
Thou by the Indian Ganges' side   5
Shouldst rubies find; I by the tide
Of Humber would complain. I would
Love you ten years before the flood,
And you should, if you please, refuse
Till the conversion of the Jews.   10
My vegetable love should grow
Vaster than empires and more slow;
An hundred years should go to praise
Thine eyes, and on thy forehead gaze;
Two hundred to adore each breast,   15
But thirty thousand to the rest;
An age at least to every part,
And the last age should show your heart.
For, lady, you deserve this state,
Nor would I love at lower rate.   20
    But at my back I always hear
Time's wingéd chariot hurrying near;
And yonder all before us lie
Deserts of vast eternity.
Thy beauty shall no more be found,   25
Nor, in thy marble vault, shall sound
My echoing song; then worms shall try
That long-preserved virginity,

And your quaint honor turn to dust,
And into ashes all my lust: 30
The grave's a fine and private place,
But none, I think, do there embrace.
    Now therefore, while the youthful hue
Sits on thy skin like morning dew,
And while thy willing soul transpires   35
At every pore with instant fires,
Now let us sport us while we may,
And now, like amorous birds of prey,
Rather at once our time devour
Than languish in his slow-chapped power.   40
Let us roll all our strength and all
Our sweetness up into one ball,
And tear our pleasures with rough strife
Through the iron gates of life:
Thus, though we cannot make our sun   45
Stand still, yet we will make him run.

Carpe diem means "seize the day." "To His Coy Mistress" presents an age-old argument in a *carpe diem* theme. What is the situation?
What contrasts does the poem present?
"Slow-chapped" means slowly chewing. "Conversion of the Jews" refers to the last judgment. Why are such things mentioned?
Is the poem essentially about love or time?

A PLEA

JOHN CIARDI

I said to her tears: "I am fallible and hungry,
and refusal is no correction and anger no meal.
Feed me mercies from the first-bread of your heart.

I have invented no part of the error it is
to be human. The least law could jail me   5
and be upheld; the least theology, damn me

and be proved. But when, ever, have I come to you
to be judged? Set me straight to your last breath,
and mine, and feed me most what I need not deserve

—or starve yourself, and starve me, and be right."

Comment on the similarities and differences between this modern *carpe diem* poem and "To His Coy Mistress," written during the seventeenth century. Has "love" changed a great deal over the centuries? Which argument do you find most convincing? Why?

THE CANONIZATION

JOHN DONNE

For God's sake hold your tongue, and let me love,
   Or chide my palsy, or my gout,
My five gray hairs, or ruined fortune, flout,
    With wealth your state, your mind with arts improve,
     Take you a course, get you a place,[1]   5
     Observe His Honor, or His Grace,
Or the King's real, or his stamped face[2]
   Contemplate; what you will, approve,
So you will let me love.

Alas, alas, who's injured by my love?   10
   What Merchant's ships have my sighs drowned?
Who says my tears have overflowed his ground?
    When did my colds a forward spring remove?
     When did the heats which my veins fill
     Add one more to the plaguy bill?[3]   15
Soldiers find wars, and lawyers find out still
   Litigious men, which quarrels move,
   Though she and I do love.

Call us what you will, we are made such by love;
   Call her one, me another fly,   20
We're tapers too, and at our own cost die,
    And we in us find the eagle and the dove.[4]
     The phoenix riddle hath more wit
     By us: we two being one, are it.
So, to one neutral thing both sexes fit.   25
   We die and rise the same, and prove
   Mysterious by this love.

[1] find yourself
[2] on coins
[3] record of plague deaths
[4] symbols of strength and purity

We can die by it, if not live by love,
  And if unfit for tombs and hearse
Our legend be, it will be fit for verse;   30
  And if no piece of chronicle we prove,
    We'll build in sonnets pretty rooms;
    As well a well-wrought urn becomes
The greatest ashes, as half-acre tombs,
  And by these hymns, all shall approve   35
  Us canonized for love:

And thus invoke us: You whom reverend love
  Made one another's hermitage;
You, to whom love was peace, that now is rage;
  Who did the whole world's soul contract, and drove   40
    Into the glasses of your eyes
    (So made such mirrors, and such spies,
That they did all to you epitomize)
  Countries, towns, courts: Beg from above
  A pattern of your love!   45

John Donne in seventeenth century England wrote both erotic love poems to his lady and deeply religious poems to God. In "The Canonization" he speaks of his love in religious terms; in "Holy Sonnet 14" (page 191) he speaks to God as if to a lover. Notice the unusual *conceits* (extended comparisons) in this poem. To what does the speaker compare himself and his lover? What other comparisons do you find?

GIRL

BARBARA MILES

girl you are a flower
very pretty growing
everything believing
and nothing knowing
        man's kick is to pluck   5
        you when you bloom
        and drop your torn-up
        petals in a lonely room

girl you are a ripe
fruit very tasty   10
understanding too slow
going under hasty

man's kick is to pick
you when you're sweet
and toss you out when   15
he's had enough to eat

girl you are a garden
full of good dirt
very hard discouraging
very easy hurt   20
    man's kick is to fill
    you full of seeds
    and plow you under when
    you sprout up weeds

girl you are a dumb   25
chick full of folly
soft heart is hard life
in this world little dolly
    kicked around you'll pick
    up what it's all about   30
    and wise up someday when
    you're all plucked out

What is the *tone* (the author's attitude toward his topic or his audience—comic, sad, ironic, sarcastic, and so on) of this poem? From what does this tone derive? Compare the tone here to that of "The Penny-candystore."

Compare this girl to Eve in "The Fall."

How does this concept of woman compare to your observations?

THE WARNING

ROBERT CREELEY

For love—I would
split open your head and put
a candle in
behind the eyes.

Love is dead in us   5
if we forget
the virtues of an amulet
and quick surprise.

What is an amulet? How does it fit here?

What is meant by the speaker's startling statement that he "would split open your head and put a candle in"? Is he, as the words may suggest, an ax murderer? How do we know?

What does the second stanza add to the poem?

AND SHE WAITING

JACK GILBERT

Always I have been afraid
of this moment:
of the return to love
with perspective.
I see these breasts   5
with the others.
I touch this mouth
and the others.
I command this heart
as the others.   10
I know exactly
what to say.

Innocence has gone
out of me.
The song.   15
The song, suddenly,
has gone out
of me.

RAPED

STUART KENT POLZIN

Canned expression giggled
    on protein-muscled chest
Cherry lipstick kissed
    binaca-freshened breath
Blue-tinted contacts   5
    brutally raped a miniskirt
Plastic hands moved slowly
    'neath a permaprest plaid shirt
Blind mechanical fingers
    caressed a form-fit, up-lift bra
And no one was surprised
    to find nothing there at all

Why is "nothing there at all"? What did the speaker expect to find?
What do words like *binaca-freshened* and *permaprest* suggest? How
do they contribute to the theme?
What does the poem say about love? About society in general?
Compare this poem to "And She Waiting."

IN HEAVENLY REALMS

E. E. CUMMINGS

in heavenly realms of hellas dwelt
two very different sons of zeus:
one,handsome strong and born to dare
—a fighter to his eyelashes—
the other,cunning ugly lame;   5
but as you'll shortly comprehend
a marvellous artificer

now Ugly was the husband of
(as happens every now and then
upon a merely human plane)   10
someone completely beautiful;
And Beautiful, who(truth to sing)
could never quite tell right from wrong,
took brother Fearless by the eyes
and did the deed of joy with him   15

then Cunning forged a web so subtle
air is comparatively crude;
an indestructible occult
supersnare of resistless metal:
and(stealing toward the blissful pair)   20
skilfully wafted over them-
selves this implacable unthing

next,our illustrious scientist
petitions the celestial host
to scrutinize his handiwork: 25
they(summoned by that savage yell
from shining realms of regions dark)
laugh long at Beautiful and Brave
—wildly who rage, vainly who strive;
and being finally released   30
flee one another like the pest

thus did immortal jealousy
quell divine generosity,
thus reason vanquished instinct and
matter became the slave of mind;   35
thus virtue triumphed over vice
and beauty bowed to ugliness
and logic thwarted life:and thus—
but look around you,friends and foes

my tragic tale concludes herewith: 40
soldier,beware of mrs smith

"Ugly" is Hephaestus (Vulcan), the Greek god of the forge, who was married to Aphrodite (Venus), the goddess of love and "Beautiful" in this poem. Aphrodite was caught in a love affair with Ares (Mars), the god of war and "Brave" here, by an invisible net with the strength of steel forged by her husband, and she was held up to the ridicule of all the gods. What theme can be inferred from the retelling of this myth?

LETTER TO MY SISTER

ANNE SPENCER

It is dangerous for a woman to defy the gods;
To taunt them with the tongue's thin tip,
Or strut in the weakness of mere humanity,
Or draw a line daring them to cross;
The gods who own the searing lightning,   5
The drowning waters, the tormenting fears,
The anger of red sins . . .
Oh, but worse still if you mince along timidly—
Dodge this way or that, or kneel, or pray,
Or be kind, or sweat agony drops,   10
Or lay your quick body over your feeble young,
If you have beauty or plainness, if celibate,
Or vowed—the gods are Juggernaut,
Passing over each of us . . .
    Or this you may do: 15
Lock your heart, then quietly,
And, lest they peer within,
Light no lamp when dark comes down.
Raise no shade for sun,
Breathless must your breath come thru,   20
If you'd die and dare deny
The gods their godlike fun!

Who are "the gods"?

What picture does this poem give of the relationship between the sexes?

What is the tone?

YESTERDAY

MICHAEL POGLIANO

yesterday your hair
blew
   & wind whipped sunshine
   through each hour
spring green   5
played
upon our running
& laughter drew
   shadows passing
   growing longer   10
then
you were gone
   just a jet plane
   emptiness here in the air
   & me humming a soft song   15
   all across an empty parking lot

UNTITLED

SHARON BUCK

I think it was because you laughed
going away, and blew a kiss,
while I,
intent on leaving you,
saw nothing moisture soft to save,   5
at last.
In gusts of barren deserts arrogant
dewy white moth wings
disintegrate.

ERAT HORA

EZRA POUND

"Thank you, whatever comes." And then she turned
And, as the ray of sun on hanging flowers
Fades when the wind hath lifted them aside,
Went swiftly from me. Nay, whatever comes
One hour was sunlit and the most high gods   5
May not make boast of any better thing
Than to have watched that hour as it passed.

The last three poems all dealt with separation, often sad. What is the tone in each? How does language contribute to tone?

MEMORIES

CATHERINE CHO WOO

Memories
   old
      faded
         yellow
           Memories.   5

A smile
   a touch
      a whisper
         of
      yesteryear,   10
         faraway.

In the background,
   yet never gone.
They were thrown away,
   yet they stayed.

For they really belong to us!

How do words like *old, faded,* and *yellow* help to establish the tone? What is the tone?
How can something that is "thrown away" (line fourteen) "stay"?

from MODERN LOVE

GEORGE MEREDITH

1

By this he knew she wept with waking eyes:
That, at his hand's light quiver by her head,
The strange low sobs that shook their common bed
Were called into her with a sharp surprise,
And strangled mute, like little gaping snakes,   5
Dreadfully venomous to him. She lay
Stone-still, and the long darkness flowed away
With muffled pulses. Then, as midnight makes
Her giant heart of Memory and Tears
Drink the pale drug of silence, and so beat   10
Sleep's heavy measure, they from head to feet
Were moveless, looking through their dead black years
By vain regret scrawled over the blank wall.
Like sculptured effigies they might be seen
Upon their marriage tomb, the sword between;   15
Each wishing for the sword that severs all.

2

It ended, and the morrow brought the task.
Her eyes were guilty gates, that let him in
By shutting all too zealous for their sin:
Each sucked a secret, and each wore a mask.   20
But, oh, the bitter taste her beauty had!
He sickened as at breath of poison-flowers:
A languid humor stole among the hours,
And if their smiles encountered, he went mad,
And raged deep inward, till the light was brown   25
Before his vision, and the world, forgot,
Looked wicked as some old dull murder spot.
A Star with lurid beams, she seemed to crown
The pit of infamy: and then again
He fainted on his vengefulness, and strove   30
To ape the magnanimity of love,
And smote himself, a shuddering heap of pain.

3

This was the woman; what now of the man?
But pass him. If he comes beneath a heel,
He shall be crushed until he cannot feel,   35

Or, being callous, haply till he can.
But he is nothing—nothing? Only mark
The rich light striking out from her on him!
Ha! what a sense it is when her eyes swim
Across the man she singles, leaving dark   40
All else! Lord God, who mad'st the thing so fair,
See that I am drawn to her even now!
It cannot be such harm on her cool brow
To put a kiss? Yet if I meet him there!
But she is mine! Ah, no! I know too well   45
I claim a star whose light is overcast:
I claim a phantom woman in the Past.
The hour has struck, though I heard not the bell!

16

In our old shipwrecked days there was an hour,
When in the firelight steadily aglow,
Joined slackly, we beheld the red chasm grow
Among the clicking coals. Our library bower
That eve was left to us: and hushed we sat   245
As lovers to whom Time is whispering.
From sudden-opened doors we heard them sing:
The nodding elders mixed good wine with chat.
Well knew we that Life's greatest treasure lay
With us, and of it was our talk. "Ah, yes!   250
Love dies!" I said: I never thought it less.
She yearned to me that sentence to unsay.
Then when the fire domed blackening, I found
Her cheek was salt against my kiss, and swift
Up the sharp scale of sobs her breast did lift—   255
Now am I haunted by that taste! that sound!

17

At dinner, she is hostess, I am host.
Went the feast ever cheerfuller? She keeps
The Topic over intellectual deeps
In buoyancy afloat. They see no ghost.   260
With sparkling surface-eyes we ply the ball:
It is in truth a most contagious game:
HIDING THE SKELETON, shall be its name.
Such play as this the devils might appall!
But here's the greater wonder: in that we,   265
Enamored of an acting nought can tire,
Each other, like true hypocrites, admire;
Warm-lighted looks, Love's ephemeridae,[1]

[1] insects which live one day only

Shoot gayly o'er the dishes and the wine.
We waken envy of our happy lot.   270
Fast, sweet, and golden, shows the marriage knot.
Dear guests, you now have seen Love's corpse-light shine.

50

Thus piteously Love closed what he begat: 785
The union of this ever diverse pair!
These two were rapid falcons in a snare,
Condemned to do the flitting of the bat.
Lovers beneath the singing sky of May,
They wandered once; clear as the dew on flowers: 790
But they fed not on the advancing hours:
Their hearts held cravings for the buried day.
Then each applied to each that fatal knife,
Deep questioning, which probes to endless dole.
Ah, what a dusty answer gets the soul   795
When hot for certainties in this our life!—
In tragic hints here see what evermore
Moves dark as yonder midnight ocean's force,
Thundering like ramping hosts of warrior horse,
To throw that faint thin line upon the shore!   800

These sixteen-line sonnets (a rare form, as sonnets commonly have fourteen lines) are from |a *sonnet sequence* (a number of sonnets that together tell a story or are closely related) of fifty poems. They trace the breaking of a marriage. The six poems that appear here cover essential points of the narrative. What happens? How are these happenings depicted? Pay particular attention to diction.

How does the poet manage to inject emotion into the story?
What images are associated with the couple?

GOODBYE

PETER DAVISON

A sailing cloud of pipe smoke wrecked itself
Against the wall. He watched its noiseless crash
And waited among the memories of the room
For the expected footstep on the stair.
Last meeting. What would be said he knew,   5
Had known for months. The words had turned to stone,
And now were to be quarried, shaped, laid in place,
Wrenched from where they had rested all this time.

A rattle at the door downstairs, the sound
Of feet ascending, steps with a slump in them,   10
As though the climber's bones had turned to chalk.
Then for the hundredth time, the handle turned,
The door opened before her, she came in.
Her smile gleamed out as she took off her coat,
And his eyes drank deep, thirst even now unquenched   15
For hair as tawny as a winter hillside,
Eyes blue and vague, hands with a milkmaid's grip,
Legs strong for walking. Beneath her clothes he could
Remember breast and belly soft as fruit—
Yet slack for him. Fruit never gave itself   20
Less eagerly to a hungry mouth than she did.

"Well." With another smile she took her seat,
Shook out her hair, waited as usual.
Her cigarette filled silence till he spoke.
"You came . . . We had to talk . . . It's time . . . You know?"   25
"Yes," she said rapidly, "I guess it is."
He'd spoken it all before—the give and take
Of weary argument, nothing to win or lose—
But now, with a growing chill, he knew his mind
Because her true indifference had come through.   30
All he had wanted was to win a debate,
Persuade her against her will she wanted him,
Make her admit it even though she lied.

The silence fell like snowflakes, and the swirl
Grew thicker, stronger, deeper. In his head   35
A frightened hammering began. This wasn't the way
He had expected it to be at all!
She wasn't there; she simply was not interested.
No argument—she did not care to argue.
Yet she was kind, and in her kindness waited   40
Till he should let her go. He came and tried
To touch her, touch her with his hands, since words
Had lost their power with her. But her flesh
Was hearkening to something else. He felt
He could shriek at her, and still she would be deaf;   45
Could strike her, and her body feel no blow.

Yet she was crying, staring straight ahead.
He knew the tears were not for him. "All right,"
He said, "I'm sorry this is how it ends.
But there's no point going on," knowing that he   50
Had to pretend to take the final step
Although they both knew it was long since taken.

A kiss upon the cheek, as for an older brother,
And she was gone. Her steps went slowly down
One flight, then headlong down a second, like   55
A bird who finds the door of its cage left open.
The street door slammed behind her, and he heard
The sound of it for hours, it seemed, because
The clang of hammers started in his head
Again, and now he knew they would not stop.   60

Compare "Goodbye" to "Modern Love." Both poems deal with the breaking of a marriage; one was written fairly recently, while the other was written during the nineteenth century. Which is which? How do you know?

from THE WASTE LAND

T. S. ELIOT

At the violet hour, when the eyes and back
Turn upward from the desk, when the human engine waits
Like a taxi throbbing waiting,
I Tiresias, though blind, throbbing between two lives,
Old man with wrinkled female breasts, can see   5
At the violet hour, the evening hour that strives
Homeward, and brings the sailor home from sea,
The typist home at teatime, clears her breakfast, lights
Her stove, and lays out food in tins.
Out of the window perilously spread   10
Her drying combinations touched by the sun's last rays,
On the divan are piled (at night her bed)
Stockings, slippers, camisoles, and stays.
I Tiresias, old man with wrinkled dugs
Perceived the scene, and foretold the rest—   15
I too awaited the expected guest.
He, the young man carbuncular, arrives,
A small house agent's clerk, with one bold stare,
One of the low on whom assurance sits
As a silk hat on a Bradford millionaire.   20
The time is now propitious, as he guesses,
The meal is ended, she is bored and tired,
Endeavours to engage her in caresses
Which still are unreproved, if undesired.
Flushed and decided, he assaults at once;   25
Exploring hands encounter no defence;

His vanity requires no response,
And makes a welcome of indifference.
(And I Tiresias have foresuffered all
Enacted on this same divan or bed;   30
I who have sat by Thebes below the wall
And walked among the lowest of the dead.)
Bestows one final patronising kiss,
And gropes his way, finding the stairs unlit . . .

   She turns and looks a moment in the glass,   35
Hardly aware of her departed lover;
Her brain allows one half-formed thought to pass:
"Well now that's done: and I'm glad it's over."
When lovely woman stoops to folly and
Paces about her room again, alone,   40
She smoothes her hair with automatic hand,
And puts a record on the gramophone.

Tiresias was a blind prophet of Thebes, according to Greek mythology. He was said to be both male and female, and therefore, as one story goes, he was called upon to settle an argument between Zeus and Hera over whether a man or a woman derives the most pleasure from the sexual act. Hera, Zeus's wife, maintained that man did, and when Tiresias contradicted her she struck him blind. Zeus gave him the gift of prophecy to compensate for his blindness.

Define *carbuncular* and *propitious*.

These lines are from a much longer poem by Eliot, *The Waste Land,* which deals with the sterility of modern society. How is that theme reflected here?

What is the tone?

Line thirty-nine alludes to Goldsmith's "Woman," written during the eighteenth century.

WOMAN

OLIVER GOLDSMITH

When lovely woman stoops to folly,
   And finds too late that men betray,
What charm can soothe her melancholy?
   What art can wash her tears away?

The only art her guilt to cover,   5
   To hide her shame from every eye,

To give repentance to her lover,
And wring his bosom is—to die.

A VALEDICTION: FORBIDDING MOURNING

JOHN DONNE

As virtuous men pass mildly away,
   And whisper to their souls to go,
Whilst some of their sad friends do say
   The breath goes now, and some say, No;

So let us melt, and make no noise,   5
   No tear-floods, nor sigh-tempests move,
'Twere profanation of our joys
   To tell the laiety our love.

Moving of th' earth brings harms and fears,
   Men reckon what it did and meant;   10
But trepidation of the spheres,
   Though greater far, is innocent.[1]

Dull sublunary lovers' love
   (Whose soul is sense) cannot admit
Absence, because it doth remove   15
   Those things which elemented it.

But we by a love so much refined
   That our selves know not what it is,
Inter-assured of the mind,
   Care less, eyes, lips, and hands to miss.   20

Our two souls therefore, which are one,
   Though I must go, endure not yet
A breach, but an expansion,
   Like gold to airy thinness beat.

If they be two, they are two so   25
   As stiff twin compasses are two;
Thy soul, the fixt foot, makes no show
   To move, but doth, if th' other do.

[1] harmless

And though it in the center sit,
   Yet when the other far doth roam,   30
It leans and harkens after it,
   And grows erect, as that comes home.

Such wilt thou be to me, who must
   Like th' other foot, obliquely run;
Thy firmness draws my circle just,   35
   And makes me end where I begun.

Define *valediction, profanation, laiety, trepidation, sublunary, obliquely.*

A *metaphysical conceit* (an extended and startling comparison) rules this poem. What is it?

Is the speaker going to die? How do you know?

4
Poetry, Subject, and Diction

When poetry is mentioned we often think first of hearts and flowers, moon and June, and other "appropriate" poetic topics. This attitude, however, views poetry much too narrowly. To be sure, much poetry—good and bad—has been written about such things, but many fine poems have also been written about "unpoetic" topics. Here is an example.

AUTO WRECK

KARL SHAPIRO

Its quick soft silver bell beating, beating,
And down the dark one ruby flare
Pulsing out red light like an artery,
The ambulance at top speed floating down
Past beacons and illuminated clocks   5
Wings in a heavy curve, dips down,
And brakes speed, entering the crowd.
The doors leap open, emptying light;
Stretchers are laid out, the mangled lifted
And stowed into the little hospital.   10
Then the bell, breaking the hush, tolls once,
And the ambulance with its terrible cargo
Rocking, slightly rocking, moves away,
As the doors, an afterthought, are closed.

We are deranged, walking among the cops   15
Who sweep glass and are large and composed.

One is still making notes under the light.
One with a bucket douches ponds of blood
Into the street and gutter.
One hangs lanterns on the wrecks that cling,   20
Empty husks of locusts, to iron poles.

Our throats were tight as tourniquets,
Our feet were bound with splints, but now,
Like convalescents intimate and gauche,
We speak through sickly smiles and warn   25
With the stubborn saw of common sense,
The grim joke and the banal resolution.
The traffic moves around with care,
But we remain, touching a wound
That opens to our richest horror.   30
Already old, the question Who shall die?
Becomes unspoken Who is innocent?
For death in war is done by hands;
Suicide has cause and stillbirth, logic;
And cancer, simple as a flower, blooms.   35
But this invites the occult mind,
Cancels our physics with a sneer,
And spatters all we knew of denouement
Across the expedient and wicked stones.

Some people will protest vehemently that "Auto Wreck" deals with an "unpoetic" subject and, therefore, is bad poetry. Certainly no one would deny that its subject is far from pleasant. At the same time, however, anyone who drives today's freeways immediately recognizes how well Shapiro has captured all the aspects of a common tragedy in a few well-chosen words. Shapiro not only shows us the scene itself—the smashed cars, the blood, the ambulance, the curious crowds, the policemen attempting to untangle the mess—but he also conveys to the reader exactly how the witnesses feel about the wreck—from the sudden shock of the unexpected tragedy to the final questioning: "Why did this have to happen? Who was at fault?"

Feeling is probably the single most important element that separates poetry from prose in an account of such an event. Consider, for a moment, how the morning newspaper might carry the story of this particular wreck:

LOCAL ACCIDENT CLAIMS VICTIMS: Traffic was tied up for three hours by a fatal crash on the Harbor Freeway at ten P.M. last night. Two cars were so completely demolished against iron poles that it took policemen three hours to clean up the debris, disburse gathering crowds, untangle heavy traffic, and get the road back into normal operation again. Causes of the accident are being investigated. Names of victims are being withheld until notification of next of kin.

The essential facts all appear in the news report, but very little of the mixed horror, grief, and accusation is present. In his poem, however, Shapiro takes all of the facts from the news report and ties them together with feeling by selecting words carefully for both their denotative and connotative values. While it is true that the bells of an ambulance may indeed seem to "beat," connotatively they reflect the beating hearts of the victims pumping their life-blood into ponds on the street. Everything in the poem adds to the image of broken bodies: the "ruby flare . . . pushing out red light like an artery," the "ponds of blood" in the street that the policeman tries to wash away, the cars that resemble "empty husks of locusts," the spectators' throats that are "tight as tourniquets," their feet that feel as if they are "bound with splints," and their mental and emotional "wound" that "opens to our richest horror." You would probably not choose this poem with its unpleasantly realistic details to read at bedtime to your younger sister, nor would your grandmother care to have you recite it to her Thursday afternoon sewing circle, but it fills the bill as a fine poem about an important topic which we would all rather ignore.

Besides the deft handling of language, there is another good reason for the success of "Auto Wreck": the poem does not rely on a *stock response* (a response evoked from the unsophisticated reader by traditional symbols and attitudes like mother love, the flag, and carefree childhood) for its impact, as do advertisements and political slogans. "In the Firelight" is a poem that does rely on stock response:

IN THE FIRELIGHT

EUGENE FIELD

The fire upon the hearth is low,
   And there is stillness everywhere,
   And, like wing'd spirits, here and there
The firelight shadows fluttering go.
And as the shadows round me creep,   5

   A childish treble breaks the gloom,
   And softly from a further room
Comes: "Now I lay me down to sleep."

And, somehow, with that little pray'r
  And that sweet treble in my ears,   10
  My thought goes back to distant years,
And lingers with a dear one there;
And as I hear my child's amen,
  My mother's faith comes back to me—
  Crouched at her side I seem to be,   15
And mother holds my hands again.

Oh, for an hour in that dear place—
  Oh, for the peace of that dear time—
  Oh, for that childish trust sublime—
Oh, for a glimpse of mother's face!   20
Yet, as the shadows round me creep,
  I do not seem to be alone—
  Sweet magic of that treble tone
And "Now I lay me down to sleep!"

Field uses in his poem very little *concrete language* (specific language —as opposed to abstract—that evokes images of something real that can be perceived by the senses). Notice how Shapiro *did* use concrete language. For his effect Field relies almost entirely on stock responses toward mother love, fireside scenes, and childish innocence. As a result, his poem carries far less impact than it might.

Occasionally, a very good poet employs stock response for ironic or comic effect (see *irony*, page 106), as cummings does in this poetic *parody* (burlesque) of a political speech:

NEXT TO OF COURSE GOD

E. E. CUMMINGS

"next to of course god america i
love you land of the pilgrims' and so forth oh
say can you see by the dawn's early my
country 'tis of centuries come and go
and are no more what of it we should worry   5
in every language even deafanddumb
thy sons acclaim your glorious name by gorry
by jingo by gee by gosh by gum
why talk of beauty what could be more beaut-
iful than these heroic happy dead   10
who rushed like lions to the roaring slaughter

they did not stop to think they died instead
then shall the voice of liberty be mute?"

He spoke.   And drank rapidly a glass of water

   Cummings crowds so many patriotic clichés into so few lines that his
speaker appears ridiculous and says absolutely nothing. The poem
neither praises nor ridicules true patriotism. It does ridicule the kind
of politician who speaks almost entirely in chauvinistic clichés in an
attempt to appear a true patriot worthy of election.
   When a poet relies too heavily on stock response and clichés, degenera-
tion into pure *sentimentality* (an overindulgence in emotion unwarranted
by the content) is often the result. Sentimentality overlooks the real com-
plexity of human relations. It often gushes and tear-jerks, dealing in tri-
vialities. In short, it oversimplifies. To see the difference between an
overly sentimental treatment and a skillful treatment of a topic, we have
only to look at two poems on the same topic—the speaker's aging mother:

MY MOTHER'S HANDS

ANONYMOUS

Such beautiful, beautiful hands!
   They're neither white nor small;
And you, I know, would scarcely think
   That they were fair at all.
I've looked on hands whose form and hue   5
   A sculptor's dream might be;
Yet are those wrinkled, aged hands
   Most beautiful to me.

Such beautiful, beautiful hands!
   Though heart were weary and sad,   10
These patient hands kept toiling on,
   That the children might be glad;
I always weep, as looking back
   To childhood's distant day,
I think how those hands rested not,   15
   When mine were at their play.

Such beautiful, beautiful hands!
   They're growing feeble now,

For time and pain have left their mark
  On hands, and heart, and brow.   20
Alas! alas! the nearing time,
  And the sad, sad day to me,
When 'neath the daisies, out of sight,
  These hands will folded be.

But oh, beyond this shadow land,   25
  Where all is bright and fair,
I know full well these dear old hands
  Will palms of victory bear;
Where crystal streams through endless years
  Flow over golden sands,   30
And where the old grow young again,
  I'll clasp my mother's hands.

TO MY MOTHER

GEORGE BARKER

Most near, most dear, most loved and most far,
Under the window where I often found her
Sitting as huge as Asia, seismic with laughter,
Gin and chicken helpless in her Irish hand,
Irresistible as Rabelais, but most tender for   5
The lame dogs and hurt birds that surround her,—
She is a procession no one can follow after
But be like a little dog following a brass band.
She will not glance up at the bomber, or condescend
To drop her gin and scuttle to a cellar,   10
But lean on the mahogany table like a mountain
Whom only faith can move, and so I send
O all my faith, and all my love to tell her
That she will move from mourning into morning.

The first of the two poems relies completely on a topic guaranteed to evoke an emotional response from the unsophisticated reader—his mother's careworn hands. (After all, few things are more sacred in our society than motherhood!) Note that the poet never gives us an actual verbal picture of these hands—he only tells us what they are like. He never shows us their wrinkles and gnarled knuckles, or lets us feel their roughness so we can decide for ourselves. In a sense, he insults our intelligence. He forces us to act upon an ingrained belief that all mothers sacrifice for their children and are usually unappreciated by them until too late—true in some cases, perhaps, but by no means in all. Human beings—mothers included—are far more complex than that! Mothers incline to be human, with all the human foibles. Few achieve the perfection that this speaker assigns to his mother. Her delineation remains shadowy; we discover nothing about her except that her hands have worked hard for many years and are now growing feeble. Left unanswered are such questions as, At what has she worked? Farming? Pioneering? Weaving? Raising fifteen children? Washing thousands of dishes in Brand X detergent that roughens one's hands beyond repair? The mother never becomes more than a stereotype. As a result, the poem itself is trite and expressionless, hardly deserving a place on a Mother's Day card.

Now let's turn to the second poem. The previously trite topic becomes meaningful in the hands of George Barker. Although we may not know such a mother intimately, Barker's appears before us full-blown and truly human in all her Irish glory. Barker also loves his mother dearly. She, too, has been a dedicated mother. But she is unique! She is fat and jolly ("huge as Asia, seismic with laughter"); she thoroughly enjoys gastronomic delights ("gin and chicken helpless in her Irish hand"); she is firm in her convictions ("She will not glance up at the bomber, or condescend /To drop her gin and scuttle to a cellar," and "only faith can move" her); and she has a soft heart for "lame dogs and hurt birds" and, by implication, children. Her death will indeed be mourned by her children, but with the knowledge that such a warm and vibrant being can look forward only to a blissful and bright eternity ("she will move from mourning into morning"). As Barker individualizes his mother more than the mother of "My Mother's Hands," he also universalizes her. As *universality* (see page 2) characterizes all good poetry and is an important reason why Shakespeare's works continue to live after hundreds of years, it helps Barker's mother "live" because her peculiarities can be observed daily in others. In short, George Barker's poem sketches a vibrant and breathing subject and at the same time makes his central point clear. It is by far the better of the two poems.

Poetic *diction* (word choice), like poetic subject, often differs from what the unsophisticated reader *thinks* it should be. Many readers consider the use a certain words in a poem taboo (as they did certain topics). In a sense, this misconception remains from the past when *decorum* (using that which is proper to a subject, character, or event) dictated that only a certain style of diction and certain topics were proper for poetry. Although we no longer demand "poetic" diction in poetry, decorum still rules to some extent. Now, however, the word choice available to the poet is considerably richer. The criterion has become simply that the language of the poem should fit the subject and the meaning to be conveyed.

Hence, we find a great variety of dictions, from the most formal to the most informal, represented in good modern poetry. *Formal diction* (elevated, often somewhat oratorical language used in academic writing and formal communication of any kind) such as John Dryden used is comparatively rare in today's poetry:

from ABSALOM AND ACHITOPHEL

JOHN DRYDEN

In pious times, ere priestcraft did begin,
Before polygamy was made a sin;
When man on many multiplied his kind,
Ere one to one was cursedly confined;
When nature prompted and no law denied   5
Promiscuous use of concubine and bride;
Then Israel's monarch after Heaven's own heart,
His vigorous warmth did variously impart
To wives and slaves; and, wide as his command,
Scattered his Maker's image through the land.   10

Today *informal diction* (language used by most educated people in everyday speech and ordinary writing) is more common in poetry. The following poem by William Carlos Williams demonstrates this level of usage:

A COLD FRONT

WILLIAM CARLOS WILLIAMS

This woman with a dead face
has seven foster children
and a new baby of her own in
spite of that. She wants pills

for an abortion and says,   5
Uh hum, in reply to me while
her blanketed infant makes
unrelated grunts of salutation.

She looks at me with her mouth
open and blinks her expressionless   10
carved eyes, like a cat
on a limb too tired to go higher

from its tormentors. And still
the baby chortles in its spit
and there is a dull flush   15
almost of beauty to the woman's face

as she says, looking at me
quietly, I won't have any more.
In a case like this I know
quick action is the main thing.   20

Good poetry sometimes contains not only *colloquial language* (conversational language used in everyday speech by everyone) but also *slang* (new meanings attached to old words and newly coined words not yet universally accepted).

"SEE IT WAS LIKE THIS"

LAWRENCE FERLINGHETTI

See
    it was like this when
            we waltz into this place
a couple of Papish cats
            is doing an Aztec two-step   5
And I says
        Dad let's cut
But then this dame
        comes up behind me see
            and says   10
        You and me could really exist
Wow I says
        Only the next day
        she has bad teeth
        and really hates   15
                poetry

In short, as long as the diction fits the purpose and subject of the poem, the poet may safely choose whatever words he pleases.

The poet, then, has an infinite range of topics at his command because no topic is considered "unpoetic" today. With extreme care he chooses his words for both their denotative and connotative values to display his topic to best advantage. The successful poet chooses concrete diction that appeals to at least one of the five senses of the reader over abstract or general words. The language and the topic he chooses, in addition to figures of speech, imagery, and sound patterns (which we will examine in subsequent chapters), make up the poet's *style* (a combination of the poet's ideas and his individual way of expressing them).

AFTERTHOUGHTS

1. Are any topics inappropriate for poetry? Why?
2. Define *decorum* in your own words. To what extent must decorum be observed in poetry? Why?
3. Distinguish between connotation and denotation. Give examples.
4. What is sentimentality? Why should it be avoided in poetry? When would it be appropriate?
5. Define *diction*.
6. Discuss in detail how subject and diction work together in the poems in this chapter.
7. Choose a poem from Chapter 5 and show how and with what degree of success the poet employs diction.

5
Man and the Establishment

DEEP INSIDE WALLET

SCOTT KINNEY

Deep inside wallet
my Social Security card
cries out to be heard.

Many words, both good and bad, have been heard recently about the Establishment. In general, this great, shadowy entity has been viewed by those past thirty as The Way of Life and by youth as The Enemy. Here, however, we shall view it as neither friend nor foe, but shall use the term simply to refer to society or Western culture in general.

The Establishment is the city in all its guises, from Wallace Stevens's "Common Life" to Michael Pogliano's "San Juan." The Establishment is more than a landscape, however. It is also what man himself has become within his self-made environment, from the cop who "slumps alertly" on Ralph Pomeroy's "Corner" to the people trapped in Blair Allen's "Maze." The Establishment embodies the many feelings (real and imagined) of superiority, aloofness, subservience, and guilt promoted by society and represented in poems like "Southern Mansion" and "from pigeons to people." The Establishment encompasses the perverted concern with materialism that forces us to pounce like spiders upon entrapped victims, as in John Ciardi's "The Hard Sell," and to cry out "I should have been a pagan," as in "The World Is Too Much With Us." The Establishment insists on *thing* worship, as the poems about the machine tell us. Finally, on the positive side, the Establishment also causes us to question all its ills, as Bonnie Buchanan does in "Accomplishment" and Bert Almon in "A Housewife Looks at the Poor."

The Establishment as represented here, then, is the society that man falls victim to, struggles against, questions, and, we hope, ultimately improves.

THERE ARE MANY TRADES

EVGENIJ VINOKUROV

(Translated by Vytas Dukas)

There are many trades.
The hunter has to hunt
The carpenter
        has to gouge
With a router,   5
Puffing and blowing;
These craftsmen have to arch their backs
With nothing to lean on.
The cosmonaut
Stepping into the night   10
          —vanishes . . .

But what does it take to be a poet?
His fate is rather sad
He does not have, by God, a trade.
He may be young or old,   15
Skill matters not at all! . . .

The whole essence is to touch
With fingers some stranger's naked soul.

What is meant by the analogy between a poet and a craftsman? Is it a true analogy? Why?

What can be inferred from lines thirteen through sixteen? From the final two lines?

THE COMMON LIFE

WALLACE STEVENS

That's the down-town frieze,
Principally the church steeple,
A black line beside a white line;
And the stack of the electric plant,
A black line drawn on flat air.   5

It is a morbid light
In which they stand,
Like an electric lamp
On a page of Euclid.

In this light a man is a result,   10
A demonstration, and a woman,
Without rose and without violet,
The shadows that are absent from Euclid,
Is not a woman for a man.

The paper is whiter   15
For these black lines.
It glares beneath the webs
Of wire, the designs of ink,
The planes that ought to have genius,
The volumes like marble ruins   20
Outlined and having alphabetical
Notations and footnotes.
The paper is whiter.
The men have no shadows
And the women have only one side.   25

What is a frieze?
Why should an electric lamp on a page of Euclid be a morbid light?
Why should a man be a result or a demonstration in this light? Why do
the men have no shadows and the women only one side?
What is Stevens saying about life?

SAN JUAN

MICHAEL POGLIANO

San Juan sea city
speaking an old tongue
to those who pass
you wrap me in
high Spanish flavor   5
    —yes
how helpless love becomes
cobblestone sideways
black iron cannon
white beaches mating   10
    green coral-warmed ocean
with you
to see an old friend
i journied in darkness
to   15
whore rows
of crazy sailors
& liquor-flowing
    steel band rhythms
    glowing in neon   20
    below the oldness
looking through
all the world's faces
to rum-toast obscurity
    cornered   25
soon on northern bent waves
i drift apart
leaving my virginity
to one of your
    dusty shelves   30

This poem also deals with a city, in this case a specific city. Compare
and contrast it with "Common Life."

Its images are particularly interesting. Consider them carefully. What
does each add to the total poem?

THE STORY OF ISAAC

LEONARD COHEN

The door it opened slowly
   My father he came in
   I was nine years old
And he stood so tall above me
   Blue eyes they were shining   5
   And his voice was very cold.
Said, "I've had a vision
   And you know I'm strong and holy
   I must do what I've been told."
So he started up the mountain   10
   I was running he was walking
   And his ax was made of gold.

The trees they got much smaller
   The lake a lady's mirror
   We stopped to drink some wine   15
Then he threw the bottle over
   Broke a minute later
   And he put his hand on mine.
Thought I saw an eagle
   But it might have been a vulture,   20
   I never could decide.
Then my father built an altar
   He looked once behind his shoulder
   He knew I would not hide.

You who build the altars now   25
   To sacrifice these children
   You must not do it any more.
A scheme is not a vision
   And you never have been tempted
   By a demon or a god.   30
You who stand above them now
   Your hatchets blunt and bloody,
   You were not there before.
When I lay upon a mountain
   And my father's hand was trembling   35
   With the beauty of the word.

And if you call me brother now
   Forgive me if I inquire
   Just according to whose plan?

When it all comes down to dust   40
    I will kill you if I must
    I will help you if I can.
When it all comes down to dust
    I will help you if I must
    I will kill you if I can.   45
And mercy on our uniform
Man of peace or man of war—
The peacock spreads his fan.

What important *allusion* (reference to something outside the lyric) is used in this poem? What does it contribute to meaning?

Who is the "father"? Who is the speaker? Is is possible that they have multiple identities in this lyric? Why?

What do you suspect may be the poet's intent? What makes you think so? How well has he made his point?

MORNING AT THE WINDOW

T. S. ELIOT

They are rattling breakfast plates in basement kitchens,
And along the trampled edges of the street
I am aware of the damp souls of housemaids
Sprouting despondently at area gates.

The brown waves of fog toss up to me   5
Twisted faces from the bottom of the street,
And tear from a passer-by with muddy skirts
An aimless smile that hovers in the air
And vanishes along the level of the roofs.

What picture of city life does this poem give you? What specific things contribute to the picture?

What is the central purpose of the poem?

CANCIÓN DE LAS HORMIGAS

PAUL BLACKBURN

Today makes 20 days
that some ants follow the same route
    across 2 of these steps
    never varying from the line.
Always this same line of ants   5
across the same 2 steps.
They may even be the same ants,
tho this would make a difference:
if the line budged one centimeter
         it would make a difference.   10

And I do not know what the job is
or when it will be finished.

Why should a poem about ants be included in this chapter? What do
the ants probably symbolize?
    Why would it make a difference if these were the same ants or if the
line budged one centimeter?
    Would it make a difference if the speaker did know what the job is
or when it will be finished? Why?

THE MAZE

BLAIR H. ALLEN

I

Madness.
Mad massiveness.
Squares within squares.
Nightmares within nightmares.
Walkways crisscrossing,   5
Running in every direction.
Multitudes marching
In computer precision
Through chilled channels,
Into blind alleys, and out again,   10
Tromping together
In a swollen river,

Increasing with every year,
Rushing toward a deadline somewhere.

II

Pausing on a stairway,   15
We stood together,
She and I,
At break time's high tide,
Those desired words,
A flow of give and take,   20
Hearts pulsing in consensus,
Eyes locked in mental embrace,
A serene, warm island
Surrounded by ice-masked torrents
Flooding past.   25

III

Upon the grey wall,
A white-faced machine
Reminding with relentless rhythm that
Time did not belong to us.
Its numerical cold stare   30
Insisting we concern ourselves with
Prim thoughts and destinations.
Its black, spear-shaped hands
Demanding in a silent scream that
We join the stream   35
She mumbled "test" in tensioned tone,
Edging from me, nervously,
Impatient schedules nagging, pulling.
Her parting look—a neon blink
As the swift current   40
Swept her away,
Pouring down the stairs
And out of sight.

IV

My mind confused,
Myself swallowed up   45
By the swollen river,
Carried quickly to the outside cold.
Around me, the lonely eyes,
The frozen mouths, the icy grips
Upon recording books.   50
Coughs fill the winter air.

Bundled forms hunch
Against the falling snow,
Huffing frosty clouds.
Legions of feet,   55
Drumming the pace,
Crush the snow to slush
Upon the walk,
Plodding onward, onward.

This poem depicts the individual being swallowed by society. What kind of society is it? How do you know?

Compare and contrast the four sections of the poem, particularly section II with the others. What do the similarities and differences suggest?

What do the last five lines suggest?

What does the repetition in the final line suggest? Notice the sound patterns throughout the poem. What do they contribute to the effect?

SOUTHERN MANSION

ARNA BONTEMPS

Poplars are standing there still as death
And ghosts of dead men
Meet their ladies walking
Two by two beneath the shade
And standing on the marble steps.   5

There is a sound of music echoing
Through the open door
And in the field there is
Another sound tinkling in the cotton:
Chains of bondmen dragging on the ground.   10

The years go back with an iron clank,
A hand is on the gate,
A dry leaf trembles on the wall.
Ghosts are walking.
They have broken roses down   15
And poplars stand there still as death.

NIGGERTOWN

THOMAS WOLFE

Below him in the valley,
Across on the butte,
The smoky lamps of Niggertown
Flared in the dusk.

Faint laughter, rich, jungle-wild,   5
Welled up from hived darkness.
He heard lost twangling notes,
The measured thump
Of distant feet.

Beyond, above,   10
More far than all,
The rapid wail of sinners
In a church.

"Southern Mansion" was written by a contemporary Negro poet. "Niggertown," written by a contemporary white novelist, originally appeared as prose and was later arranged as a poem. Compare and contrast the two poems.

A HOUSEWIFE LOOKS AT THE POOR

BERT ALMON

I have seen the poor.
I am not blind.
I see them in magazines,
A mother and hungry children.
I am moved to send a check.   5
But, that woman,
She looks sturdy enough.
Why doesn't she find a job,
Feed those children herself?

Turn the page. Spring fashions.   10
The blue silk shift tied casually
At the throat, huge silk peonies

Muffle the ears. A silk shift,
Casually tied, at the throat.
Silk peonies muffle the ears.   15

What do the contrasts contribute to the total effect of this poem?
Why is the information about current fashions repeated in the last
stanza? What does the variation in this repetition suggest?
What is the central purpose of the poem?

JUVENILE HALL

SHARON BUCK

I see the children
locked in hallways
by one by one of rooms
and periodic lights
with cold reflections   5
of the superficial color
and the yellow-night
glow of squares to
mock their private
(no not here) sleeping.   10

Perpendiculars and
flats and downs in
two converging lines,
uniform, expectable,
accomplishing a motion   15
and an end
and pressing back
away from the
empty corridor
the fetid   20
fecund
fluidity of
vermin.

I pray for crevices
and oozing life.   25

How is juvenile hall pictured? What does this depiction suggest?
The final image of the poem is somewhat repulsive. How appropriate

is it? Why should one pray for "crevices and oozing life"? What does the prayer suggest in reference to the rest of the poem? What does the poet probably mean by "crevices and oozing life"?

CORNER

RALPH POMEROY

The cop slumps alertly on his motorcycle,
Supported by one leg like a leather stork.
His glance accuses me of loitering.
I can see his eyes moving like fish
In the green depths of his green goggles.   5

His ease is fake. I can tell.
My ease is fake. And he can tell.
The fingers armored by his gloves
Splay and clench, itching to change something.
As if he were my enemy or my death,   10
I just stand there watching.

I spit out my gum which has gone stale.
I knock out a new cigarette—
Which is my bravery.
It is all imperceptible: 15
The way I shift my weight,
The way he creaks in his saddle.

The traffic is specific though constant.
The sun surrounds me, divides the street between us.
His crash helmet is whiter in the shade.   20
It is like a bull ring as they say it is just before
    the fighting.
I cannot back down. I am there.

Everything holds me back.
I am in danger of disappearing into the sunny dust.
My levis bake and my T-shirt sweats.   25

My cigarette makes my eyes burn.
But I don't dare drop it.

Who made him my enemy?
Prince of coolness. King of fear.

Why do I lean here waiting?   30
Why does he lounge there watching?

I am becoming sunlight.
My hair is on fire. My boots run like tar.
I am hung-up by the bright air.
Something breaks through all of a sudden,   35
And he blasts off, quick as a craver,
Smug in his power; watching me watch.

What kind of person is the speaker? How does his experience compare
to your experiences with policemen?
Discuss the diction used in "Corner."
What is the poem's central purpose?

IN ORDER TO

KENNETH PATCHEN

Apply for the position (I've forgotten now for what) I had
to marry the Second Mayor's daughter by twelve noon. The
order arrived at three minutes of.

I already had a wife; the Second Mayor was childless: but I
did it.   5

Next they told me to shave off my father's beard. All right.
No matter that he'd been a eunuch, and had succumbed in
early childhood: I did it, I shaved him.

Then they told me to burn a village; next, a fair-sized town;
then, a city; a bigger city; a small, down-at-heels country;   10
then one of "the great powers"; then another (another, an-
other)—In fact, they went right on until they'd told me to
burn up every man-made thing on the face of the earth! And
I did it, I burned away every last trace, I left nothing, nothing
of any kind whatever.   15

Then they told me to blow it all to hell and gone! And I blew
it all to hell and gone (oh, didn't I) . . .

Now, they said, put it back together again; put it all back the
way it was when you started.

Well . . . it was my turn to tell *them* something! Shucks,
I didn't want any job that bad.

What discrepancy do you find in the first five lines? What other discrepancies do you find in the poem? How does the central purpose arise from these discrepancies?
What does the poem say about society in general? About man in particular?

MALCOLM X, TALKING TO THE CITY:

GERALD BUTLER

"Take a walk in my head
where dew could stroke your ankles
and where there are
names to give small animals
the rainbows   5
of whose invisible flight you hear.
You could hunt them perhaps
with the wide trees
of Africa around you
and with your dreams made of leaves,   10
of mud, of the sky between ruffled feathers,
all around you:
antelope would come.
The season for antelope would come,
filling the air with honor.   15
All breaths could be caught together
in the gathering and the fire
kept transparent by the stars.

Take a walk in my black head,
heave back the rainbow, hack   20
the plain to acres
till I spit all the dream out.
Breathe on the plain and burn it off
till I vomit up the shame
sweet as the dawn there is in hell   25
when the ghosts of the animals
pass through your white hands."

Who was Malcolm X? Why should he talk to the city?
He speaks of a strange variety of things: rainbows, antelope, stars, fire,

shame, and hell. Why? What do they and what he says about them suggest?

What does he mean by "Take a walk in my head"?

HARLEM

LANGSTON HUGHES

What happens to a dream deferred?
    Does it dry up
    like a raisin in the sun?
    Or fester like a sore—
    And then run?   5
    Does it stink like rotten meat?
    Or crust and sugar over—
    like a syrupy sweet?

    Maybe it just sags
    like a heavy load.   10

    Or does it explode?

THE HARD SELL

JOHN CIARDI

The spider in its office of tuned strings
Waits at a dream's end for a rumor's twitch.
Manny waits for the phone to ring. It rings.
He pounces and devours the son-of-
    a-bitch.

SALUTATION

EZRA POUND

O generation of the thoroughly smug
    and thoroughly uncomfortable,
I have seen fishermen picnicking in the sun,
I have seen them with untidy families,
I have seen their smiles full of teeth   5
    and heard ungainly laughter.

And I am happier than you are,
And they were happier than I am;
And the fish swim in the lake
and do not even own clothing.   10

Who are "the generation of the thoroughly smug"? What relationship
is established between them, the fishermen, the fish, and the speaker?
What made the speaker happier than "the generation of the thor-
oughly smug"? What does this imply about human relationships?
Who is happiest of all? Why?

THE WORLD IS TOO MUCH WITH US

WILLIAM WORDSWORTH

The world is too much with us; late and soon,
Getting and spending, we lay waste our powers:
Little we see in Nature that is ours;
We have given our hearts away, a sorbid boon!
The Sea that bares her bosom to the moon;   5
The winds that will be howling at all hours,
And are up-gathered now like sleeping flowers;
For this, for everything, we are out of tune;
It moves us not.—Great God! I'd rather be
A Pagan suckled in a creed outworn;   10
So might I, standing on this pleasant lea,
Have glimpses that would make me less forlorn;
Have sight of Proteus rising from the sea;
Or hear old Triton blow his wreathèd horn.

What does the title of Wordsworth's poem mean?
Does he advocate paganism?
Is this poem as relevant today as it was 150 years ago?

FROM PIGEONS TO PEOPLE

ALFRED K. WEBER

through experiments we endeavour
to make pigeons press a lever,
if possible, whenever
they are hungry and deprived.

combined with the animals' yearning 5
the lever which helps in earning
some food is aim of classically learning
from where the food can be derived.

pressing the lever makes a winner
and keeps a pigeon from getting thinner 10
in its box named after skinner.
at which it finally arrives.

the crumbs it gets, however,
are never enough to sever
the habit of pushing the lever 15
ever again in order to survive—
from crumb to crumb
from pigeon to people
from day to day

pushing the levers of time clocks 20
in the mornings
and in the afternoons
to be free to
push the levers of vending machines
(in the evenings) 25
which yield:

gas for tomorrow's ride to work
(to be in school, office, factory on time,
at seven, eight o'clock, or nine),
peppermint crumbs for a fresh breath 30
for the stale mouths of the sleepless and hungry,
condoms for the hygienic execution
of passions,
cigarettes for a sense of being alive, now
and for cancer later, 35
games for forgetting ourselves
in our leisure time too:

our daily bread
of hope for enough bread
for tomorrow, 40
of fear to be unfed
for not pushing the lever
in the mornings
and in the afternoons.

What relationship have pigeons to people?

What purpose do lines seventeen through nineteen serve?
Notice how the form of the poem changes. What does this suggest?

ON ROMAN TRAFFIC

JOHN CIARDI

What is this raging in the streets of Rome?
The poor have all won lotteries and become
by Fiat, Phaetons. Earth and sky, beware!
Zeus, have you one last thunderbolt? Are you there?

Phaeton was the son of Helios, the Greek god of the sun. He persuaded his father to allow him to drive the chariot of the sun across the sky for one day, but being weaker than Helios, Phaeton allowed the horses to run off their course and too close to the earth, almost destroying it with fire. Zeus, the king of the gods, became angered and killed Phaeton with a thunderbolt.

A FIRE-TRUCK

RICHARD WILBUR

Right down the shocked street with a siren-blast
That sends all else skittering to the curb,
Redness, brass, ladders and hats hurl past,
    Blurring to sheer verb,

Shift at the corner into uproarious gear   5
And make it around the turn in a squall of traction,
The headlong bell maintaining sure and clear,
    Thought is degraded action!

Beautiful, heavy, unweary, loud, obvious thing!
I stand here purged of nuance, my mind a blank.   10
All I was brooding upon has taken wing,
    And I have you to thank.

As you howl beyond hearing I carry you into my mind,
Ladders and brass and all, there to admire
Your phoenix-red simplicity, enshrined   15
    In that not extinguished fire.

What is meant by the final line in stanza I? In stanza II?
Define *nuance*.
Why is "phoenix-red" more appropriate here than blood-red or
scarlet? How does this particular color relate to the final line of the
poem?

from THE SOUL OF YOUTH—
THE FEAR OF AGE

SHARON SOSNA

The Son

The day that I tasted the richness of manhood
The soft ocean breath was whispering to me.
I ran to danger as bees fly to nectar,
Ran to the luring call of the sea.

I sought the waves as a balm to my spirit.   5
The brine in my veins was as flame to my blood.
My soul was thirsty and ripe for the dour
Taste of sea water, cool in its flood.

I dared to temper a surfboard beneath it.
I tried to harness its power 'neath my feet,   10
Taunting the breakers to crush and embrace me,
I give myself up to its wild pulsing beat.

The Father

"My son, turn away from the pulse that excites you.
No man can claim he has vanquished the sea."

The Son

"Father, fear drowned when first I was weeping.   15
The man who will conquer the ocean is me."

The sea is often used in literature as a symbol of life or of eternity. A
symbol can be both itself and something else besides; for example, a flag
is literally a piece of cloth and symbolically a country. Is the sea used
symbolically in the preceding poem?

WHILE MY GUITAR GENTLY WEEPS

GEORGE HARRISON

I look at you all see the love there that's sleeping
While my guitar gently weeps
I look at the floor and I see it needs sweeping
Still my guitar gently weeps
I don't know why nobody told you how to unfold your love   5
I don't know how some controlled you
They bought and sold you.

I look at the world and I notice it's turning
While my guitar gently weeps
With every mistake we must surely be learning   10
Still my guitar gently weeps
I don't know how you were diverted
You were perverted too
I don't know how you were inverted
No one alerted you.   15

I look at you all see the love there that's sleeping
While my guitar gently weeps
Look at you all . . .
Still my guitar gently weeps.

If you can, listen to the Beatles' recording of this lyric. Notice the
synchronization of sound and sense.
Distinguish among *diverted, perverted,* and *inverted.* Do these words
follow a logical order?
Who is probably the "you" of stanza II?

THE FALL OF ROME

W. H. AUDEN

The piers are pummelled by the waves;
In a lonely field the rain
Lashes an abandoned train;
Outlaws fill the mountain caves.

Fantastic grow the evening gowns;   5
Agents of the Fisc pursue
Absconding tax-defaulters through
The sewers of provincial towns.

Private rites of magic send
The temple prostitutes to sleep;   10
All the literati keep
An imaginary friend.

Cerebretonic Cato may
Extoll the Ancient Disciplines,
But the muscle-bound Marines   15
Mutiny for food and pay.

Caesar's double-bed is warm
As an unimportant clerk
Writes I DO NOT LIKE MY WORK
On a pink official form.   20

Unendowed with wealth or pity,
Little birds with scarlet legs,
Sitting on their speckled eggs,
Eye each flu-infected city.

Altogether elsewhere, vast   25
Herds of reindeer move across
Miles and miles of golden moss,
Silently and very fast.

Define *pummel, Fisc, absconding, provincial, literati, cerebretonic, extoll.*
What images arise from the poem? What do they imply?
Contrast the final two stanzas with the other stanzas.
What is the significance of the birds and the vast herds of reindeer?

LONG-LEGGED FLY

WILLIAM BUTLER YEATS

That civilization may not sink,
Its great battle lost,
Quiet the dog, tether the pony
To a distant post;

Our master Caesar is in the tent   5
Where the maps are spread,
His eyes fixed upon nothing,
A hand under his head.
Like a long-legged fly upon the stream
His mind moves upon silence.   10

That the topless towers be burnt
And men recall that face,
Move most gently if move you must
In this lonely place.
She thinks, part woman, three parts a child,   15
That nobody looks; her feet
Practice a tinker shuffle
Picked up on a street.
Like a long-legged fly upon the stream
Her mind moves upon silence.   20

That girls at puberty may find
The first Adam in their thought,
Shut the door of the Pope's chapel,
Keep those children out.
There on that scaffolding reclines   25
Michael Angelo.
With no more sound than the mice make
His hand moves to and fro.
Like a long-legged fly upon the stream
His mind moves upon silence.   30

What relationships do you find among the three stanzas?
What are the "topless towers" referred to in stanza II?
Who is "she" of stanza II?
What is the "Pope's chapel"?
The minds of three people are said to "move upon silence." How does
the meaning of this phrase vary from stanza to stanza?
What is the poem about?

ACCOMPLISHMENT

BONNIE BUCHANAN

Ah ha,
and what have we here?
A wicked plot of warped wasteland.

Man and the Establishment

Parched ruins of temples,
   and homes   5
   and dreams.
Rivers of blood,
   polluted with flesh and bone.
The stench of hatred smoldering in
   every wretched corner.   10
Earth?
Oh, come now.
Where are those
   blue skies
   and green trees   15
   and red roses
      and . . .
Smoke.
Smoke remains.

Hey you! Mankind!   20
Stand up,
     and take your bow!

    Poems may be written in a number of tones: gay, sad, bitter, ironic, and so on. What is the tone of this poem? What specific things contribute to this tone?

6
Poetry
and Image

Now that we have read and thought about several poems (Chapters 1, 3, and 5), and have discovered how to analyze a poem (Chapter 2) and what kinds of topics and language we can reasonably expect to find in good poetry (Chapter 4), let us turn to the images of a poem. Imagery, mentioned briefly before, often takes an important role in poetry and can hardly be ignored in a discussion of any other aspect of the poem. Imagery breathes life into a poem. It forces the reader to see, hear, smell, taste, and touch imaginatively and to react emotionally and intellectually to the poet's descriptions and ideas. Imagery allows the reader to experience vicariously the sensations of the poet when he confronted his subject first-hand.

Imagery works in a variety of ways. Usually it arises from descriptions or figures of speech that appeal to the senses, emotions, and intellect of the reader and evoke imaginary pictures of something concrete. Perhaps the most common form of image evoked by poetry is visual: a word picture is painted for the reader. Skillful poets appeal to other senses as well. Seldom does a single poem appeal to all five senses at once, however, in the way that "Autumn" does.

TO AUTUMN

JOHN KEATS

I

Season of mists and mellow fruitfulness,
Close bosom-friend of the maturing sun;

Conspiring with him how to load and bless
With fruit the vines that round the thatch-eves run;
To bend with apples the moss'd cottage-trees,   5
And fill all fruit with ripeness to the core;
To swell the gourd, and plump the hazel shells
With a sweet kernel; to set budding more,
And still more, later flowers for the bees,
Until they think warm days will never cease,   10
For Summer has o'er-brimm'd their clammy cells.

II

Who hath not seen thee oft amid thy store?
Sometimes whoever seeks abroad may find
Thee sitting careless on a granary floor,
Thy hair soft-lifted by the winnowing wind;   15
Or on a half-reap'd furrow sound asleep,
Drows'd with the fume of poppies, while thy hook
Spares the next swath and all its twined flowers:
And sometimes like a gleaner thou dost keep
Steady thy laden head across a brook;   20
Or by a cyder-press, with patient look,
Thou watchest the last oozings hours by hours.

III

Where are the songs of Spring? Ay, where are they?
Think not of them, thou hast thy music too,—
While barred clouds bloom the soft-dying day,   25
And touch the stubble-plains with rosy hue;
Then in a wailful choir the small gnats mourn
Among the river sallows,[1] borne aloft
Or sinking as the light wind lives or dies;
And full-grown lambs loud bleat from hilly bourn;   30
Hedge-crickets sing; and now with treble soft
The red-breast whistles from a garden-croft;
And gathering swallows twitter in the skies.

The poem's controlling image is nature—a particularly sensuous nature (appealing to the reader's senses). Keats evokes images of the fruition of autumn through *sight* (the thatched cottage surrounded by overloaded trees and vines and flowers around which the bees fly, the "barred clouds," the full-grown lambs, and so on); *hearing* (the buzzing of the bees, the wind, the "wailful choir" of gnats, the loud bleat of the lambs,

[1] shallows

Poetry and Image

the singing of the crickets, the whistling of the robin, and the twittering of the swallows); *touch* (the warmth of the "maturing sun," the clammy cells" of the hives, the softness of the "winnowing wind"); *smell* (the flowers, the "fume of poppies," the cider oozing from the press); and *taste* (the ripeness of the fruit, the "sweet kernel" of the hazel nuts, the cider). A master of sensuous imagery, Keats's prime tool is figurative language.

When the poet uses *figurative language* (a fresh, new manner of expression), he departs from the ordinary in construction, word order, meaning, or a combination of these. You and I unconsciously use figurative language daily. When you ask your roommate to turn down his stereo because your head is splitting, for example, you are speaking figuratively; you do not mean that your head is literally crumbling apart, but that you have a headache. This is only one example of the many kinds of figurative language. The most common poetic figures of speech have special names: antithesis, apostrophe, hyperbole, simile, metaphor, personification, synecdoche, metonymy, and irony.

Antithesis is fairly simple to grasp. It is characterized by strong contrasts: a balancing of opposing words, clauses, sentences, and ideas against one another for effect. By the strong contrasts between *err* and *forgive* and between *human* and *divine,* for example, Alexander Pope employed antithesis in the line, "To err is human; to forgive, divine."

Less frequently used than most other figures of speech, *apostrophe* (addressing an inanimate object as if it were alive, a dead or absent person as if he were present) is also fairly simple to understand. Exemplifying apostrophe is Wordsworth's address to long-dead Milton:

> Milton! thou shouldst be living at this hour:
> England hath need of thee, . . .

More common than either apostrophe or antithesis is *hyperbole* (an extreme exaggeration used in both poetry and prose either to heighten effect or to provide comic effect). Most of us use hyperbole from time to time in ordinary speech: "It's raining cats and dogs!" "It must be a zillion degrees outside today!" "I'm so hungry that I could eat a horse!" A classic use of poetic hyperbole is found in Andrew Marvell's "To His Coy Mistress" (see page 50 for the entire poem):

> Had we but world enough, and time, . . .
> An hundred years should go to praise
> Thine eyes, and on thy forehead gaze;
> Two hundred to adore each breast,
> But thirty thousand to the rest;
> An age at least to every part,
> And the last age should show your heart.

The speaker begins his age-old argument to his lady—urging her to love him now before they are both too old—with flattery. He tells her that his love for her is so great that were he capable, he would woo her throughout eternity, an age given to praising each part of her. Certainly no love could be more extravagant! Because he remains mortal, though, such a love exceeds his reach. His flattery, then, is a vast exaggeration, or hyperbole.

Simile is another figure of speech used frequently in both poetry and prose: "She is as fresh as a daisy." "He is as clumsy as a bull in a china shop." "Your eyes are like precious gems." Simile directly expresses similarity between two things, usually by employing the words *like* or *as;* it, too, is used by Marvell in his proposal to his lady:

> Now let us sport us while we may,
> And now, *like* amorous birds of prey,
> Rather at once our time devour. . . .

The speaker desires an active love, rather than the passive affair that his coy lady has insisted upon, and what could be more active than "amorous" and voracious birds?

Differing slightly from simile and probably the most frequently used figure of speech of all, *metaphor* makes either an implicit or an explicit comparison without using comparative words such as *like* and *as*. In some respects we think metaphorically. Many of our utterances, particularly our slang expressions, unconsciously employ metaphor: "That test was a bear!" "He's a skunk!" "She's a doll!" These are all direct metaphors (metaphors that make explicit comparisons). But when Marvell says, "Rather at once our time devour/Than languish in his slow-chapped power," he uses an implicit (or indirect) metaphor. He implies a comparison between time and a slowly chewing creature that devours reluctant lovers. Sometimes, then, a metaphor states emphatically that one thing equals another; more commonly, however, it simply implies the equality.

A special form of metaphor in which an important part of something (a part most associated with the whole) is used to represent the whole, or the whole is used to stand for the part, is called a *synecdoche*. The following lines from "The Love Song of J. Alfred Prufrock" (see page 16 for the complete poem) demonstrate synecdoche:

> I should have been a pair of ragged claws
> Scuttling across the floors of silent seas.

The "ragged claws" stand for the entire animal (probably a crab or a lobster). Notice how well this figure helps to characterize Prufrock, a timid soul who suffers from the scrutiny of others. He wishes that he, like the crustacean, could hide at the bottom of the ocean where he would not be constantly on display to the world.

Closely related to metaphor and image is *symbol*, which evokes a concrete reality but suggests at the same time another level of meaning. An image means exactly what it seems to; a metaphor means something other than it appears to on the surface; and a symbol means both what it appears to mean and more than it appears to mean on the surface. Common symbols include the flag (literally, a piece of varicolored cloth; symbolically, a country), the White House (literally, a large white house; symbolically, the president of the United States), or the press (literally, a printing press; symbolically, all printed material).

Poetry sometimes contains symbols that are more or less unique to particular poets. In the following poem, for example, a turtle which at one time stayed entirely in its shell but now is emerging to make its presence felt symbolizes the American Negro.

THE EMANCIPATION OF
GEORGE-HECTOR

(a colored turtle)

MARI E. EVANS

George-Hector
. . . is
spoiled.
formerly he stayed
well up in his
shell . . . but now
he hangs arms and legs
sprawlingly
in a most languorous fashion . . .
head reared back
to
be
admired.

he didn't use to
talk . . .
but
he does now.

More conventional literary symbols are the sea (eternity), the journey (life), and the rose (variously, love, a woman, and Christ).

Personification lends human attributes to animals, ideas, and inanimate objects. When we insist that our dog "talks" to us, for example, we are actually personifying him. Keats's "Ode to Autumn" personifies Autumn. This is perhaps most easily seen in the second stanza, where Keats pictures Autumn as a reaper:

> Who hath not seen thee oft amid thy store?
>   Sometimes whoever seeks abroad may find
> Thee sitting careless on a granary floor,
>   Thy hair soft-lifted by the winnowing wind;
> Or on a half-reap'd furrow sound asleep,
>   Drows'd with the fume of poppies, while thy hook
>   Spares the next swath and all its twined flowers:
> And sometimes like a gleaner thou dost keep
>   Steady thy laden head across a brook;
>   Or by a cyder-press, with patient look,
>   Thou watchest the last oozings hours by hours.

Obviously, the season Autumn does not literally sit on the floor, nor does it have hair for the wind to blow. It cannot be lulled to sleep by the fume of poppies as it scythes down the ripened crop, and it cannot watch anything, much less a cyder-press. But all these characteristics together give the spirit of Autumn life. Through the personification the reader vicariously experiences the essence of an autumn day.

Another fairly common figure of speech, *metonymy*, substitutes a closely associated word for the word itself. Like so many other modes of figurative language, metonymy often appears in everyday speech. For example, we might say that *"poverty* lives in the ghettos," meaning that poor people live in the ghettos, or that *"wealth* lives on Snob Hill," meaning that rich people live there. Returning to Marvell's poem, we find a metonymy in the second-to-last line:

> Thus, though we cannot make our sun
> Stand still, yet we will make him run.

"Sun," closely associated with the reckoning of time, is a metonymy for time itself, the main concern of the entire poem.

Perhaps the most difficult of all figures of speech, even though we often use it in ordinary conversation, is *irony*. Irony deals in discrepancy and exists in three forms: verbal irony, dramatic irony, and irony of situation.

Verbal irony, the simplest of the three varieties of irony, consists of a discrepancy between what the speaker says and what he means. It may have been storming for the past three days; the streets are flooded; reluctantly you have arisen at six AM from a cosy bed, choked down burned toast and lukewarm coffee, and sloshed for an hour through knee-deep puddles only to find that school has been closed because of the weather. You turn to a companion and comment, "Great day!" Unless you are part platypus, you probably mean exactly the opposite of what you say. You are being ironic. The speaker in the following poem ironically maintains his constancy as a lover:

OUT UPON IT!

SIR JOHN SUCKLING

Out upon it! I have loved
    Three whole days together;
And am like to love three more,
    If it prove fair weather.

Time shall molt away his wings,   5
    Ere he shall discover
In the whole wide world again
    Such a constant lover.

But the spite on 't is, no praise
    Is due at all to me: 10
Love with me had made no stays
    Had it any been but she.

Had it any been but she,
    And that very face,
There had been at least ere this   15
    A dozen in her place.

"I am a constant lover," the speaker insists, but what he tells us about his "constancy" contradicts what he so adamantly maintains. We have good reason to suspect that he talks with his tongue in his cheek; thus, verbal irony.

Dramatic irony differs slightly from verbal irony in that the discrepancy is not between what the speaker says and what he means, but between what the speaker says and what the author means. Dramatic irony originated with Greek drama, in which the audience was familiar with the plot of the tragedy before the play began. There was a discrepancy between what the stage character thought would happen and what the audience *knew* would happen. The following short poem gives an example of dramatic irony in poetry.

EARTH

(with apologies to *The New Yorker*)

JOHN HALL WHEELOCK

"A planet doesn't explode of itself," said drily
The Martian astronomer, gazing off into the air—
"That they were able to do it is proof that highly
Intelligent beings must have been living there."

The Martian astronomer makes one observation about Earth (that it takes intelligent beings to blow up a planet), while the speaker who is quoting the Martian actually says something entirely different about Earth (man is not so intelligent, after all, if he insists on blowing up his planet). The discrepancy between the two viewpoints results in dramatic irony.

Irony of situation involves a discrepancy between the appropriate or anticipated circumstance and the actual situation. Every automobile driver will recognize the irony of situation in "Ambition":

AMBITION

MORRIS BISHOP

I got pocketed behind 7X–3824;
He was making 65, but I can do a little more.
I crowded him on the curves, but I couldn't get past,
And on the straightaways there was always some truck
    coming fast.
Then we got to the top of a mile-long incline
And I edged her out to the left, a little over the white line,
And ahead was a long grade with construction at the bottom,
And I said to the wife, "Now by golly I got'm!"
I bet I did 85 going down the long grade,
And I braked her down hard in front of the barricade,
And I swung in ahead of him and landed fine
Behind 9W–7679.

Irony, a tremendously powerful tool, can make a situation seem comic, as Suckling uses it in his poem, or make a strong point, as Wheelock uses it in "Earth"—and sometimes both at the same time, as in Bishop's poem. The ability to recognize irony marks intelligence and sophistication, for its subtleties often go unrecognized by the immature or careless reader who takes every printed word literally.

Occasionally, a careless reader confuses irony with sarcasm, which often uses irony as a tool. The difference between sarcasm and irony lies in their intent. Sarcasm usually intends cruelty and hurt, while irony can be considered neither cruel nor kind. It can be both gentle and bitter. Used skillfully, irony adds great depth and subtlety to a work. The ironic author has his tongue in his cheek and figuratively winks his eye to let his reader know that he actually means the opposite of what he says. The sarcastic author has no tongue in cheek, no wink. He makes it clear that he means what he says. To illustrate the difference between irony and sarcasm, assume for a moment that the most important social event of the year approaches. You know two girls: Beth, an extremely beautiful and popular girl, and Marge, who has a flaming case of acne, reeking halitosis and body odor, fifty extra pounds of flesh, buck teeth, stringy hair, and a personality to match. Talking to your friends, you say exactly the same thing about each girl: *"She'll* never get a date for the Spring Fling!" When you are talking about Beth you probably have a slight twinkle in your eye, because from previous knowledge of Beth and her activities you are sure that she will have many possible dates from which to choose. You are being ironic. When you are talking about Marge, though, your tone will differ slightly. You are absolutely serious. Your knowledge of Marge tells you that no boy can stand being close enough to her to ask her for a date. You are being sarcastic.

Figurative language is one of many methods the poet uses to achieve vivid imagery. *Allusion* (reference to something outside of the poem) is another. Although allusion can be made to virtually anything, the most common allusions in literature are to mythology, Shakespeare, and the Bible.

MYTHOLOGY

LEDA AND THE SWAN

WILLIAM BUTLER YEATS

A sudden blow: the great wings beating still
Above the staggering girl, her thighs caressed

By the dark webs, her nape caught in his bill,
He holds her helpless breast upon his breast.

How can those terrified vague fingers push   5
The feathered glory from her loosening thighs?
And how can body, laid in that white rush,
But feel the strange heart beating where it lies?

A shudder in the loins engenders there
The broken wall, the burning roof and tower   10
And Agamemnon dead.
                    Being so caught up,
So mastered by the brute blood of the air,
Did she put on his knowledge with his power
Before the indifferent beak could let her drop?   15

How well Yeats's powerful poem deals with the theme of violence begetting violence! The theme could easily be missed, though, by a reader unfamiliar with the myth of Leda, to which the poem alludes. Leda, the wife of Tyndareus, king of Sparta, was raped by Zeus, king of the Greek gods, who assaulted her in the shape of a swan (Zeus could assume any shape he wished). From this violent union resulted Castor, Pollux, Helen, and Clytemnestra. Helen was later kidnapped by Paris of Troy, the event which led to the Trojan War, the sacking of Troy by Agamemnon (Clytemnestra's husband and Helen's brother-in-law), and ultimately to the murder of Agamemnon by Clytemnestra. Yeats alludes to the myth to demonstrate how one violent act (the rape of Leda) leads to other violent acts. The final question—"Did she put on his knowledge with his power?" —expands the allusion to universal significance: will people *ever* learn from violence?

SHAKESPEARE

from THE WASTE LAND

T. S. ELIOT

The Chair she sat in, like a burnished throne,
Glowed on the marble, where the glass
Held up by standards wrought with fruited vines
From which a golden Cupidon peeped out
(Another hid his eyes behind his wing)   5
Doubled the flames of sevenbranched candelabra

Reflecting light upon the table as
The glitter of her jewels rose to meet it,
From satin cases poured in rich profusion;
In vials of ivory and coloured glass   10
Unstoppered, lurked her strange synthetic perfumes,
Unguent, powdered, or liquid—troubled, confused
And drowned the sense in odours; stirred by the air
That freshened from the window, these ascended
In fattening the prolonged candle-flames,   15
Flung their smoke into the laquearia,
Stirring the pattern on the coffered ceiling.
Huge sea-wood fed with copper
Burned green and orange, framed by the coloured stone,
In which sad light a carved dolphin swam.   20
Above the antique mantel was displayed
As though a window gave upon the sylvan scene
The change of Philomel, by the barbarous king
So rudely forced; yet there the nightingale
Filled all the desert with inviolable voice   25
And still she cried, and still the world pursues,
"Jug Jug" to dirty ears.
And other withered stumps of time
Were told upon the walls; staring forms
Leaned out, leaning, hushing the room enclosed.   30
Footsteps shuffled on the stair.
Under the firelight, under the brush, her hair
Spread out in fiery points
Glowed into words, then would be savagely still.

   "My nerves are bad to-night. Yes, bad. Stay with me.   35
"Speak to me. Why do you never speak? Speak.
   "What are you thinking of? What thinking? What?
"I never know what you are thinking. Think."

Eliot alludes to several things, but most specifically to Enobarbus's description of Cleopatra as she floats down the Nile on her resplendent royal barge:

from ANTONY AND CLEOPATRA, II, ii

WILLIAM SHAKESPEARE

The barge she sat in, like a burnish'd throne,   195
Burn'd on the water: the poop was beaten gold;

Purple the sails, and so perfumed that
The winds were love-sick with them; the oars were silver,
Which to the tune of flutes kept stroke, and made
The water which they beat to follow faster,   200
As amorous of their strokes. For her own person,
It beggar'd all description: she did lie
In her pavilion—cloth-of-gold of tissue—
O'er-picturing that Venus where we see
The fancy outwork nature: on each side her   205
Stood pretty dimpled boys, like smiling Cupids,
With divers-colour'd fans, whose wind did seem
To glow the delicate cheeks which they did cool,
And what they undid did.

Enobarbus describes Cleopatra as a woman who is both sensuous and sensual. All of her surroundings—the golden throne, the purple and perfumed sails, the music, and so on—contribute to what she proves herself to be in the play. Eliot, alluding to this famous description, implies some of Cleopatra's grandeur, but notice how he tempers it with a less vital society—"*synthetic* perfumes" that "*troubled, confused* and *drowned* the sense," smoking candles that give off "*sad* light," art works that tell of mythological wonders of the past which have become only "*withered* stumps of time," and the empty silence of the room and the people in it—to characterize something slightly different: a neurotic woman whose senses are drowned in the sensuality of a decadent society. Knowledge of the source of the allusion again contributes to a fuller understanding of what the poet is saying.

THE BIBLE

THE LATEST DECALOGUE

ARTHUR HUGH CLOUGH

Thou shalt have one God only; who
Would be at the expense of two?
No graven images may be
Worshipped, except the currency.
Swear not at all; for, for thy curse   5
Thine enemy is none the worse.
At church on Sunday to attend
Will serve to keep the world thy friend.
Honor thy parents; that is, all
From whom advancement may befall.   10

Thou shalt not kill; but need'st not strive
Officiously to keep alive.
Do not adultery commit;
Advantage rarely comes of it.
Thou shalt not steal; an empty feat,   15
When it's so lucrative to cheat.
Bear not false witness; let the lie
Have time on its own wings to fly.
Thou shalt not covet, but tradition
Approves all forms of competition.   20

The sum of all is, thou shalt love,
If anybody, God above:
At any rate shall never labor
More than thyself to love thy neighbor.

Clough obviously alludes to the Ten Commandments and all that they imply. He twists them ironically, though, to comment upon the hypocrisy of modern society, the final lines suggesting in their discrepancy that the reason for this hypocrisy is self-love.

Imagery achieved through allusion and figurative language is one of the most powerful tools available to the poet. The good poet deftly employs all kinds of allusions and figurative language—from the Bible to Shakespeare and from antithesis to simile—along with other tools such as diction, rhythm, and sound patterns to evoke the images of his poem. One important critical question in any analysis of poetry is "How does the poet employ images?"

AFTERTHOUGHTS

1. Define imagery in your own words. How does a poet create images in a poem? Can you think of other ways to create imagery?

2. In another chapter, find a poem that uses allusion. Show how allusion contributes to the total effect. What other tools does the poet use?

3. In another chapter, find a poem that uses symbolism. Describe how this tool is used.

4. Define the following figures of speech and try to find examples (other than those already given) of each: antithesis, apostrophe, hyperbole, simile, metaphor, personification, synecdoche, metonymy.

5. The excerpt from "The Waste Land" alludes to Shakespeare's *Antony and Cleopatra*. What other allusions can you find in it?

6. Define and give examples of the three kinds of irony.

7
Man and War

WHEN A MAN HATH NO FREEDOM

GEORGE GORDON, LORD BYRON

When a man hath no freedom to fight for at home,
Let him combat for that of his neighbors;
Let him think of the glories of Greece and of Rome,
And get knocked on his head for his labors.

War seems to be the eternal curse of mankind. Hardly a year has passed in human history without men waging war with one another somewhere on earth. The Norsemen saw heroic death in violent battle as the only salvation for man. The Greeks and Romans made sacrifices to war gods. Medieval knights rode off on noble quests and were often expected to die in an equally noble manner in romantically glorified battles. Religious leaders led countless men to certain death in furious wars to preserve or extend a faith. Throughout history men have forsaken everything peaceful and fruitful to carry the banner of one cause or another, told to return "with their shields or on them." But the wars of the twentieth century have a flavor entirely their own.

After World War I, we no longer find war glorified. It became evident that the "war to end all wars" had not lived up to expectations when less than twenty years later a mad ex-paperhanger threw all of Europe—and subsequently the entire world—into chaos. Disillusionment, becoming apparent years earlier, grew. All men reacted during the *unglorious* years of World War II, from the gently ironic humor of Bill Mauldin to the stalwart defiance of Winston Churchill to the ultimate horror of all civilized people at the annihilation of millions of humans in extermination camps. War had indeed lost its shine. Instead of bidding our men to come home "with their shields or on them," we silently prayed that they would return in one mental and physical piece. After the smoke had cleared, we hoped hopelessly that the end of conflict really had been reached. Korea, followed closely by Vietnam, extinguished this feeble hope in many, particularly in young people, who seemed to see, and what is more, forced others to see only too clearly the utter hellishness of war.

The cry against the brutal side of man began perhaps as early as seventeenth century Milton in his protest against "The Last Massacre in Piedmont," picked up and gained an ironic twist in Byron's "When a Man Hath No Freedom to Fight for at Home," and continued in Hardy, who probed the relevance of killing in war in "The Man He Killed." These early cries, however, are usually simply ironic or indignant. The World War I poets, on the other hand (represented here by Wilfred Owen), speak in a different tone. Owen's poems (foreshadowing his own ironic death two days before the armistice) deftly portray major unpleasantries, obscenities, bitter ironies, and most of all the pity of war.

More recent poets view the stark realities of war: the possibility of facing a meaningless death a million miles from home in "The End," the outraged horror of an atrocity in "the initiation rites at Mylai," and the bitterness of being forced to kill men like vermin in "It's Not Like Killing Men." Gone are the traces of glory perceptible even in Milton's indignant cry. Real events are now viewed through real eyes and reported in strong language, for words like *glory* and *cause* no longer ring true to poets.

WITH GOD ON OUR SIDE

BOB DYLAN

Oh, my name it is nothin',
My age it means less,
The country I come from
Is called the Midwest.
I's taught and brought up there,   5
The laws to abide,
And that land that I live in
Has God on its side.

Oh, the history books tell it,
They tell it so well,   10

The cavalries charged,
The Indians fell.
The cavalries charged,
The Indians died,
Oh the country was young   15
With God on its side.

Oh, the Spanish American
War had its day,
And the Civil War too
Was soon laid away,   20
And the names of the heroes
I's made to memorize,
With guns in their hands
And God on their side.

Oh, the First World War boys,   25
It came and it went,
The reason for fighting
I never did get.
But I learned to accept it,
Accept it with pride,   30
For you don't count the dead
When God's on your side.

When the Second World War
Came to an end,
We forgave the Germans   35
And we were friends.
Though they murdered six million
In the ovens they fried,
The Germans now too
Have God on their side.   40

I've learned to hate Russians
All through my whole life,
If another war starts
It's them we must fight.
To hate them and fear them,   45
To run and to hide,
And accept it all bravely
With God on my side.

But now we got weapons
Of the chemical dust,   50
If fire them we're forced to
Then fire them we must.

One push of the button
And a shot the world wide,
And you never ask questions   55
When God's on your side.

In a many dark hour
I've been thinkin' all this,
That Jesus Christ
Was betrayed by a kiss.   60
But I can't think for you
You'll have to decide,
Whether Judas Iscariot
Had God on his side.

So now as I'm leavin'   65
I'm weary as Hell,
The confusion I'm feelin'
Ain't no time can tell.
The words fill my head
And fall to the floor,   70
If God's on our side
He'll stop the next war.

The speaker insists that God is on the side of "right." Does he mean what he says?
What is the tone? From what does this tone emerge? Be specific.

CRYSTAL NIGHT

JOHN CIARDI

I told one devil to the end
and found no other. In his place
came day by day, the long bone round
—the race.

Came hunters scarified for God,   5
their magic twitching in their eyes,
their lances cocked for any blood
not theirs.

Came Pharaohs mounted past the world
but with their whole weight on it still.   10

In their beginning was the word
—kill.

Came sultans dappled by the rays
of their own rubies. Not quite God,
but gods enough to like God's ways   15
with blood.

Came monks in their own shadows, vowed
to rack out error, thus to save
the essence God had not allowed
a grave.   20

Came troopers in their polished meat,
too lucid to have tears to shed.
Came order, ordnance. At its feet
the dead.

Came man, alas, by right and wrong,   25
by can and will, by Hellgate slammed
his red night through, his long bone round
the damned.

Compare and contrast the first and last stanzas. How do you account
for the similarities and differences? What is the progression of events?
What "essence" had God "not allowed a grave"?
Define *scarified.*
What do the hunters, Pharaohs, sultans, monks, troopers, and man
symbolize, respectively?

THE DEAD

AUGUSTINE BOWE

Dead men keep their fingers on a trigger;
Dead men have weapons they can use.
Targets grow bigger and bigger,
Truce of all sort refuse.
If you keep listening to voices of the dead,   5
There will be no peace ever anywhere.
The sun will rise angry and red;
Night will be a dark and sullen stare.

Man and War

What is meant by the statement in line one?
Comment on the use of *refuse* in line four.
Why should there never be peace if we "keep listening to voices of the dead?"

THE LIGHT ON THE PEWTER DISH

KENNETH REXROTH

Driving across the huge bridge
Above San Francisco Bay,
The United States Navy
Anchored, rank by deadly rank,
In the water under me,   5
And over me the sky filled
With hundreds of bombing planes,
My mind wandering idly,
I was suddenly aware
That Jacob Boehme flourished   10
During the Thirty Years' War.

Jacob Boehme was a Lutheran mystic who lived from 1575 to 1624. What are the implications of the fact that he flourished during the Thirty Years' War?

ANTHEM FOR DOOMED YOUTH

WILFRED OWEN

What passing-bells for these who die as cattle?
Only the monstrous anger of the guns.
Only the stuttering rifles' rapid rattle
Can patter out their hasty orisons.
No mockeries for them from prayers or bells,   5
Nor any voice of mourning save the choirs—
The shrill, demented choirs of wailing shells;
And bugles calling for them from sad shires.

What candles may be held to speed them all?
Not in the hands of boys, but in their eyes   10
Shall shine the holy glimmers of good-byes.

The pallor of girls' brows shall be their pall;
Their flowers the tenderness of patient minds,
And each slow dusk a drawing-down of blinds.

Comment on the *alliteration* (repetition of initial consonant sounds
or closely related vowel sounds) used in this poem.
What kinds of figurative language do you find?
What is the tone?

CHILDREN IN THE SHELTER

DANIEL BERRIGAN

Imagine; three of them.

As though survival
were a rat's word,
and a rat's end
waited there at the end   5

and I must have
in the century's boneyard
heft of flesh and bone in my arms

I picked up the littlest
a boy, his face   10
breded[1] with rice (his sister calmly feeding him
as we climbed down)

In my arms fathered
in a moment's grace, the messiah
of all my tears. I bore, reborn   15

a Hiroshima child from hell.

Who is the "messiah"? What does his presence suggest? How does he
compare or contrast with our usual concept of a messiah?

[1] embroidered

FISH

DANIEL BERRIGAN

a freak's eye
a cold shoulder
a dog's mouth
a green complexion—
alas for   5
immortal longings—
to die a hero
arms locked
fervently as a lion's
about the beloved prey—   10
the world   the world!

Absurd?
You have seen me
a basket case
nailed   15
in cold blood
to the scaling board
stinking
to high heaven

no beauty   20
no comeliness
a worm
alas no man.

How do figurative language and imagery work together?
How does form contribute to the total effect?

Three poems follow for comparison and contrast. Consider ideas, images,
diction, figurative language, and form.

THE WAR IS HERE

BLAIR H. ALLEN

We're facing the fallout
Gray walls waivering
In the gray atmosphere
Grainy grit to the taste
Clogging our lungs   5
Eyes flooding blood
The gray-making machine
Stifling the free air
Mad scarlet sun sinking
Behind a lethal screen   10
Etched image in my eye
The grayness weighing
Heavy all over me
And upon sleeping you
As time shrinks slow   15
But faster than you think
Children staring hard
Accusation at you and I
While we deny the fault
Lying within ourselves   20
Settling in inactivity
Young piercing penetrations
Saying across new gaps
Don't lie to the young
For they will know   25
In the unforgiving future

from HUGH SELWYN MAUBERLEY

EZRA POUND

There died a myriad,
And of the best, among them,
For an old bitch gone in the teeth,
For a botched civilization,

Charm, smiling at the good mouth,   5
Quick eyes gone under earth's lid,

For two gross of broken statues,
For a few thousand battered books.

DULCE ET DECORUM EST

WILFRED OWEN

Bent double, like old beggars under sacks,
Knock-kneed, coughing like hags, we cursed through sludge,
Till on the haunting flares we turned our backs,
And towards our distant rest began to trudge.
Men marched asleep. Many had lost their boots,   5
But limped on, blood-shod. All went lame, all blind;
Drunk with fatigue; deaf even to the hoots
Of gas-shells dropping softly behind.

Gas! GAS! Quick, boys! An ecstasy of fumbling,
Fitting the clumsy helmets just in time,   10
But someone still was yelling out and stumbling
And flound'ring like a man in fire or lime.—
Dim through the misty panes and thick green light,
As under a green sea, I saw him drowning.

In all my dreams before my helpless sight   15
He plunged at me, guttering, choking, drowning.

If in some smothering dreams, you too could pace
Behind the wagon that we flung him in,
And watch the white eyes writhing in his face,
His hanging face, like a devil's sick of sin,   20
If you could hear, at every jolt, the blood
Come gargling from the froth-corrupted lungs
Bitten as the cud
Of vile, incurable sores on innocent tongues,—
My friend, you would not tell with such high zest   25
To children ardent for some desperate glory,
The old Lie: *Dulce et decorum est*
Pro patria mori.

The Latin is quoted from the Roman poet Horace and means "It is sweet and becoming to die for one's country." In what sense is this quotation used here?

What is the author's tone?

THE INITIATION RITES AT MYLAI

BARBARA MILES

soldier, in your armored dream
of being a man,
you enter with your blood brothers
into a village
of old men,   5
and women, and children,
and around them you draw
the fire circle
of your crazed initiation.

and you gather them together   10
into a wailing huddle,
a helpless target
composed of all your engorged
and impotent memories,
and with a jismic clench   15
of the groin,
the trigger finger,
you spray the sacrificial bodies
with iron seed.

the old man crouched toothless   20
and unsexed, you shoot,
making yourself
the surrealistic father of yourself,—
he stares at you,
begging speechless for his life,   25
and you blast bullets
of your unfulfilled genes
into his mouth.

the woman next, cowering,
her breast half-bared   30
to your rival,
you shoot in staccato ecstasy,
and when you shoot her with
a real gun,
she stays laid,   35
she convulses in the dirt,
she bleeds for you,
soldier.
she's yours.

poem might be compared and contrasted with Genesis, in fact—here an inverted Genesis, however. How does this biblical flavor affect the poem?

THE MAN HE KILLED

THOMAS HARDY

Had he and I but met
By some old ancient inn,
We should have sat us down to wet
Right many a nipperkin![1]

But ranged as infantry,   5
And staring face to face,
I shot at him as he at me,
And killed him in his place.

I shot him dead because—
Because he was my foe,   10
Just so: my foe of course he was;
That's clear enough; although

He thought he'd 'list, perhaps
Off-hand-like—just as I—
Was out of work—had sold his traps[2]—   15
No other reason why.

Yes; quaint and curious war is!
You shoot a fellow down
You'd treat if met where any bar is,
Or help to half-a-crown.   20

Pay particular attention to the diction and punctuation in this poem. How do they contribute to the total poem?

What kind of man is the speaker? How do you know? (Hardy was never a soldier: this poem illustrates the danger of assuming that the speaker of a poem is the poet himself.)

The speaker struggles with a problem. What is it?

What is the central purpose of the poem?

[1] half-pint cup
[2] tools of one's trade

THE WAR—LAST YEAR IN JUNE, THIS YEAR

ALFRED K. WEBER

But we did turn our heads to the side
at times
   in e m b r a c e s
catching sight of coasting cars
and of red roses and of chasing children   5
in the sunlight
   in e m b r a c e s
I saw our smile at them on your face
the same waving of your hand
   f a c i n g   y o u   10
and we did express exasperation at the
slaughter of children
saw their seared shoulders with
indignation and their raw, gory flesh on
puffed up bellies with fury   15
in the papers
   in e m b r a c e s
and toothless crones, haggard faces
grooved arms patched with white plaster we
saw and we agreed   20
upon compassion for the dying
   f a c i n g   b u t   e a c h   o t h e r
and we agreed upon contempt for those that
caused death and counted on dying and
cashed pains and cast planes and cast white plaster   25
   f a c i n g   b u t   e a c h   o t h e r
we would weep together
last year in June with
our lips kissing our tears
   in e m b r a c e s   30
our touching tongues conveyed our
outcries, those whispered words of
   f a c i n g   b u t   e a c h   o t h e r
fury at the death of children's laughter
enclosed by our mouths, the   35
circle of playing lips
   o u r   b a c k s   t u r n e d   u p o n   o t h e r   f a c e s

The juxtaposition of the embraces and the dead children is ironic. Why? Why is love repugnant?

What kind of person is the speaker? What indicates this?

What should we infer from this poem about people's attitudes toward war in general?

8
Poetry
and Cadence

In nature we find rhythm in the changing of the seasons, the movement of the tides, and the growth of all things; in human events we find a pendulum-like rhythmic swing between various extremes of fashion, politics, religion, and other activities; in painting rhythm is reflected in the artist's brush strokes which force our eyes to travel back and forth across the canvas; in music we find rhythm in the beat of the song which sets our foot tapping; in prose we find rhythm in the accents of individual words, in the sequence of words, and in the way the author forces us to follow his twists and turns of mind. We also find that rhythm is the cadence of poetry.

In no other art, except music perhaps, does rhythm play so important a role as in poetry. As we saw in Chapter 6, imagery breathes life into a poem. The same might be said about rhythm. The skillful poet deftly manipulates the accented and unaccented syllables of the words he chooses to breathe meaning and movement into his poem. By determining how we hear the words, rhythm reinforces the sensuous and intellectual life given to the poem by its imagery. It reinforces our intellectual understanding of the poem by setting up anticipated audio patterns, variations of which emphasize certain ideas; it reinforces emotional reaction to the poem by forcing us to speed up or slow down as we hear certain combinations of words. At times rhythm even controls visual reception of the poem as certain line and stanzaic patterns force the eye as well as the ear to supply cadence. We must see rhythm in action to understand how it works.

Most of us automatically and unconsciously respond to rhythm. We throb from toe to top hat as the drums of a marching band pass by; we anticipate the next blow of a carpenter's hammer; we detect a missed beat in our automobile engine, diagnosing the trouble if we are mechanically inclined and panicking if we are not; we mentally count the ticks of a clock during a long, sleepless night; and so on. But while we unconsciously "feel" rhythm around us, and in poetry as well when we hear it read aloud, most of us are unable to visualize the *meter* (rhythmical pattern) of an entire poem. Because understanding how the poet manipulates rhythm may contribute considerably to our comprehension of his message or of what he wants us to feel, *scansion* (marking a line of poetry to show the meter) was devised to help us make abstract, "felt" rhythm visual and concrete. Scansion is a tool that helps us determine certain things about a poem more exactly by giving us something visual to talk about more explicitly than we can discuss a feeling.

We scan a poem by reading it aloud and marking "heard" accented syllables so: ╱, and unaccented syllables so: ◡. Having done this, we mark metrical *feet* (units of two or more syllables—see page 141 for a complete list of metrical terms) in each line with a long slash, /, between each foot and *caesuras* (pauses that fall within the lines) with a double slash, //. In scanning poetry, however, we must be extremely careful not to distort a line simply for the sake of maintaining an anticipated meter. Words should be given approximately the same accents and lines approximately the same pauses that they would have in ordinary speech. The most important thing to keep in mind about scansion is that as an end in itself it is relatively unimportant, but as a tool to reveal one of the poet's methods and some of his meaning it can be invaluable.

The best way to see how meter works is probably to begin with a metrically regular poem. Many rather simple poems vary their meter very little, some not at all. Though few of these poems last, nursery rhymes and ballads (among the oldest of literary forms) are exceptions:

> Mary/ had a/ little/ lamb, ∧
> Its fleece/ was white/ as snow;
> Every/where that/ Mary/ went ∧
> The lamb/ was sure/ to go.

Notice how the accents fall at completely regular and predictable intervals. The meter is so predictable, in fact, that we soon find ourselves reciting the lines in a singsong manner, caught up more in the beat than in the words or their meaning. Upon scanning it, we find that this poem contains two kinds of metrical feet, each occurring regularly in alternate lines. In lines one and three we find four *trochees* (a foot containing an accented syllable followed by an unaccented syllable), or trochaic *tetra-*

meter (four feet to a line). Notice, by the way, that in this particular poem the missing but unconsciously supplied unaccented syllable at the end of lines one and three is indicated in scansion by a *caret* ($\wedge$). In lines two and four we find three *iambs* (a foot containing an unaccented syllable followed by an accented syllable), or iambic *trimeter* (three feet to a line). The utter simplicity and regularity of this particular poem contribute to its success as a nursery rhyme. It was meant to be recited or sung to and by small children. Hence, the simplicity of both words and meter is entirely appropriate. Even before a child can intellectually grasp the diction, he can recite the verse verbatim because of the regular meter.

The usual meter of ballads is like the meter of the nursery rhyme for much the same reason: a ballad is meant to be sung, and many were transmitted orally for many centuries before they were finally printed. A ballad usually tells a story; therefore, the regular meter, often enhanced by repetition or variation of a refrain at regular intervals, helps to unify the story as well as to mark turns in the narrative. The stanza commonly known as the *ballad stanza* (usually a *quatrain*—four lines of verse with a fixed pattern of rhyme and meter—with alternating tetrameter and trimeter lines rhyming *a b a b* or *x a x a, x* being nonrhyming lines) involves an expected pattern that is easy to remember and to repeat. Because of the expectation of metrical regularity, occasional irregularities in meter carry far more importance than they otherwise would. The old ballad "Barbara Allan" is a good case in point. Let us begin reading about half-way through, when Barbara's lover realizes that she has poisoned him (see page 47 for the entire ballad):

He turned/ his face/ unto/ the wall,   *a*

And death/ with him/ was dealin':   *b*

"Adieu,/ adieu,/ my dear/ friends all,   *a*

And be kind/ to Bar/bara Allan."   *b*

And slow/ly, slow/ly rase/ she up,   *x*

And slow/ly, slow/ly left him: *c*

And sigh/ing said/ She could/ not stay,   *x*

Since death/ of life/ had reft him.   *c*

She had/ not gane/ a mile/ but twa,   *x*

When she heard/ the dead-/bell knellin',   *a*

And ĕve/rў jŏw/ thăt thĕ dĕad-/bĕll gă'ed   x

Ĭt crĭed, "Wŏe/ tŏ Băr/băra Ăllăn!"   a

"Ŏ mŏth/ĕr, mŏth/ĕr, măke/ mў bĕd,   x

Ŏ măke/ ĭt sŏft/ ănd nărrŏw: d

Sĭnce mў/ lŏve dĭed/ fŏr mĕ/ tŏdăy,   x

Ĭ'll dĭe/ fŏr hĭm/ tŏmŏrrŏw."   d

While the meter and *stanzas* (a grouping of two or more lines that can take practically an infinite number of forms) of this ballad may resemble those in the nursery rhyme, scansion shows us something far more complex. The narrative of Barbara Allan deals typically (for a ballad) with death—in this case the murder of a young man by a girl he slighted and ultimately the suicide of that girl. Also typical of the ballad is the overall form and the repetition of the refrain with slight variations in lines four and twelve. Slight shifts of meter, however, ultimately affect our total concept of the poem. On first recitation we may sense that this ballad has perfect metrical regularity. To be sure, regularity can be found in almost every line—with a few important exceptions. Analyzed closely, the exceptions, though they do not disrupt our metrical expectations, do spotlight crucial points in the narrative and emphasize and extend meaning and feeling far beyond the denotative or connotative value of the words alone.

In "Barbara Allan" we find that the predominant foot is the iamb, with an *amphibrach* (a foot consisting of three syllables, the first and last unaccented, the middle one accented) consistently falling on the final foot of the second and fourth lines of each stanza. We also find the expected alternating tetrameter and trimeter lines. Even the rhyme scheme follows the expected pattern of the ballad. But when we look more closely, we suddenly discover that in lines four, ten, eleven, twelve, and fifteen the anticipated pattern has been challenged. Why? Generally a pattern of expectations is upset in a line of poetry for a good reason. The disruption of the metrical pattern in "Barbara Allan" is no exception to this rule.

The first of these metrical disruptions occurs in the first foot of line four. Instead of the expected iamb, we find an *anapest* (a foot consisting of two unaccented syllables followed by an accented syllable). Because such changes in meter are rarely accidental, we must take this one as a signal to look more closely at the line. Why does the poet wish to emphasize this particular line? Does it say something important? Is it perhaps a turning point in the poem?

"Ădiéu,/ ădiéu,/ my déar/ frĭends áll,

Ănd bĕ kínd/ tŏ Bár/băra Állăn."

Indeed this is a turning point in the narrative; these are the dying words of John Graeme, Barbara's lover. But notice exactly what he is saying. First he bids his friends farewell, and then—*almost as an afterthought*—he tells them to be kind to the woman who killed him! Knowing, as we do, that he knows that Barbara killed him, can we believe our ears?

Probably not. Had he simply and positively said, "Bĕ kínd/ tŏ Bár/băra Állăn" (notice how eliminating the "And" significantly throws the verse back into regular meter), we might pass quickly over his dying request and think no more about it. But the added unaccented syllable "And" not only jars the meter somewhat, calling attention to the line, but also underlines the already accented "kind." We suspect that while John may mean what he says, he is probably speaking ironically. Does he perhaps mean the opposite of what "kind" usually means? The meter justifies our suspicion. We may not be able to answer this question with certainty, but because it arouses our suspicion that more is happening in the poem than appears on the surface, the variation in meter at this crucial point of the narrative is significant enough to add extra depth to what is being said.

The other four irregular lines in these stanzas, we find, all deal with Barbara's dawning realization of the enormity of what she has done and lead to her further realization of what must become of her because of the ill deed: "I'll die for him tomorrow." Notice the words on which our attention is focused by irregularities of scansion in lines ten, eleven, twelve, and fifteen: "héard . . . déad . . . Wóe . . . lóve díed." All these words together help us experience Barbara's thoughts. She had barely left her newly dead lover ("She had not gane a mile but twa") when she heard the church bell tolling his death. The repetition of "dead-bell" in line eleven, with the added emphasis of an anapest instead of the anticipated iamb on "dead," drives the utter horror and finality of her act even further into Barbara's consciousness and into ours as well. The hopelessness of her situation becomes further apparent in the strong accent falling on "Woe" in line twelve. She realizes now that, as she states in line fifteen, more than simply a man has died—in addition, *"lóve díed"!* These are the two most heavily stressed words in the entire ballad and certainly should command our full attention. They draw maximum weight because the line begins with a *pyrrhic foot* (a foot consisting of two unaccented syllables) and ends with two regular iambs, casting "lo$\acute{v}$e di$\acute{e}$d" between the weak pyrrhic and the regular iambs in a strong *spondee* (a foot consisting of two accented syllables). Notice what would happen, had the poet decided to maintain a regular meter at this point:

M$\breve{y}$ lo$\acute{v}$e/ h$\breve{a}$s di$\acute{e}$d/ f$\breve{o}$r m$\acute{e}$/ t$\breve{o}$da$\acute{y}$.

No longer would the impact be so great, for in the original, not only has a young man died, but, implying much more, *love* has died! Barbara's ultimate realization of this tragedy is so awesome that she finds she can no longer go on living. Without love, she is already virtually dead. She asks her mother to prepare her coffin:

> "O mother, mother, make my bed,
> O make it soft and narrow:"

The implication that without love life is nothing arises from careful manipulation of meter—a manipulation that magnificently reveals both emotion and meaning in an otherwise simple poem.

Emphasizing emotion and meaning is not the only way manipulation of meter can contribute to the total effect of a poem. A poet may reinforce his topic by choosing an imitative meter as well. For example, Tennyson uses the *dactyl* (a foot consisting of an accented syllable followed by two unaccented syllables):

> H$\acute{a}$lf $\breve{a}$ l$\breve{e}$ague,/ h$\acute{a}$lf $\breve{a}$ l$\breve{e}$ague,
> H$\acute{a}$lf $\breve{a}$ l$\breve{e}$ague/ o$\acute{n}$wa$\breve{r}$d,
> $\acute{A}$ll $\breve{i}$n th$\breve{e}$/ va$\acute{l}$le$\breve{y}$/ $\breve{o}$f De$\acute{a}$th
> R$\acute{o}$de th$\breve{e}$ si$\breve{x}$/ h$\acute{u}$ndr$\breve{e}$d.
>
> "F$\acute{o}$rwa$\breve{r}$d th$\breve{e}$/ Li$\acute{g}$ht B$\breve{r}$iga$\breve{d}$e!
> Ch$\acute{a}$rge f$\breve{o}$r th$\breve{e}$/ g$\acute{u}$ns!" h$\breve{e}$ sa$\breve{i}$d.
> I$\acute{n}$t$\breve{o}$ th$\breve{e}$/ va$\acute{l}$le$\breve{y}$/ $\breve{o}$f De$\acute{a}$th
> R$\acute{o}$de th$\breve{e}$ si$\breve{x}$/ h$\acute{u}$ndr$\breve{e}$d.

Read aloud, the rhythm of this poem becomes the rhythm of the galloping hoofbeats it describes. This galloping meter not only echoes the hooves of the horses, it also moves the reader along at a pace closely resembling the frenzied charge of the men and horses in battle. Note, too, how the meter becomes irregular and slows the action in the two lines mentioning "Death": instead of two rapidly moving dactyls to the line, we find one dactyl followed by a trochee and an iamb. The stark and final abruptness of death in an otherwise furiously moving action is echoed in the abrupt shift of meter.

Emphasis and imitation are only two ways manipulated meter can enhance our enjoyment and understanding of poetry. Often the poet appeals to visual sense as well as to aural sense by his metrical arrangement of words on the page. Consider, for example, the two poems that follow, bearing identical titles and having similar themes, but written in totally different metrical forms, each of which influences our reception of the poem as a whole.

OZYMANDIAS

PERCY BYSSHE SHELLEY

I met/ a travel/ler from/ an an/tique land
Who said:/ Two vast/ and trunk/less legs/ of stone
Stand in/ the des/ert . . . Near/ them, on/ the sand,
Half sunk,/ a shat/tered vis/age lies,/ whose frown,
And wrin/kled lip,/ and sneer/ of cold/ command,   5
Tell that/ its sculp/tor well/ those pas/sions read
Which yet/ survive,/ stamped on/ these life/less things,
The hand/ that mocked/ them, and/ the heart/ that fed:
And on/ the ped/estal/ these words/ appear:
"My name/ is Oz/yman/dias, king/ of kings: 10
Look on/ my works,/ ye Might/y, and/ despair!"
Nothing/ beside/ remains./ Round the/ decay
Of that/ colos/sal wreck,/ boundless/ and bare
The lone/ and lev/el sands/ stretch far/ away.

OZYMANDIAS

GEORGE OPPEN

The five
Senses gone

138

To the one sense,
The sense of prominence

Produce an art
De Luxe.

And down town
The absurd stone trimming of the building tops

Rectangular in dawn, the shopper's
Thin morning monument.

The visual difference between these two poems is immediately apparent to us. The second poem depends heavily on this fact. Let's first look briefly at Shelley's "Ozymandias." Before we even read the words, we notice the apparent regularity of line length in Shelley's poem. Scansion shows us that the poem is a *sonnet* (a fourteen-line lyric, variously rhymed, usually written in iambic *pentameter*—five feet to a line). The fourteen lines are packed with descriptive diction telling how a ruthless dictator is outlived by his works. Epitomized in the shattered stone self-image, the works ironically reflect the king's mortality in their imperfections. Ironically, too, the common people—the traveller and the speaker of the poem—also outlive this "king of kings" and recognize his absurdity and vulnerability rather than "despair" at his power, as he had hoped that even the gods would do.

The central metrical point, however, is that the very strictness of the sonnet form forces the poet to emphasize meaning with shifts in metrical feet. Although many shifts occur, the most outstanding ones are the spondees in lines two, four, nine, and eleven. The strongly accented "twó vást" (line two) emphasizes the enormous size of the statue, and Ozymandias's former sphere of influence. But we find that this enormity has all but vanished. It now lies (again strongly accented) "hálf súnk" in the desert sands, a crumbling ruin, the strong accents emphasizing the enormity of the wreck. In the final lines the poet wishes to emphasize the relative importance of Ozymandias and his remains, so he points to the inscription on the base of the statue with strongly accented "thése wórds. The words presumably put there by order of Ozymandias himself, caution the viewer to "Lóok ón/ mý wórks,/ . . . aňd/despáir!" The strong spondees on the first two feet of the line make the command emphatic. The strong emphasis of the command—ironic because of its incongruity with its surroundings—is further underlined in the shift of meter in the next-to-last foot of line thirteen: "Ŏf thắt/cŏlŏs/săl wrĕck,/ bŏundlĕss/ ănd bắre." This shift draws attention to the present—the decaying opulence of what once was, starkly contrasted with the utter bareness of what now remains in the midst of a vast desert.

While Shelley achieves emphasis within a tightly disciplined sonnet form through variations in metrical feet, Oppen achieves his emphasis differently. Oppen's poem, which deals with essentially the same contrasts as Shelley's—here a contrast between the very rich who have lost their "five senses" to the "sense of prominence" and the common people, "the shoppers"—is written in *free verse* (nonmetrical or irregularly metrical lines). Although the poem is rhythmic (as all words are rhythmic), no set metrical pattern such as we found in the sonnet is established. Lines are irregular lengths, and no discernible rhyme scheme exists. Diction is bare and nondescriptive. Emphasis is achieved visually. Much as the painter forces the viewer's eye to follow his arrangement of details across the canvas, the poet forces the reader's eye to focus on certain details on the printed page. In fact, this poem might in one sense be termed a word picture. The break between each two-line stanza tends to emphasize the second line of each pair, in which the poet places important ideas: "Senses gone . . . sense of prominence . . . *De Luxe* . . . absurd stone trimming of the building tops . . . Thin morning monument." Contrasts stand out within the lines: the "one sense" of the very rich that is epitomized in *"De Luxe"* is opposed to the cheap imitation relegated to the common people and epitomized in the "thin morning monument." Notice, too, how the switch from one contrast to the other is signaled by punctuation: the period following italicized *"De Luxe."*

Of equal importance in Oppen's "Ozymandias" are the line lengths and their appearance on the page. Our eyes are forced to move back and forth and are drawn most emphatically to the italicized *"De Luxe"* (the shortest line of the poem), to line eight (the longest line), and to line ten (the final line). Intellect along with eye thus skips to the important points of the poem. Rhythmic emphasis is achieved in poetry not only through manipulation of our sense of hearing but also by manipulation of our sight.

The poet manipulates the reader's perception by manipulating the natural rhythm of words into metrical or nonmetrical patterns as suits his purpose or subject. At one time he uses meter to emphasize, at another to imitate, at still another to guide the reader's eye to important ideas by special arrangement of words on the printed page. These examples give us only a small sample of how a poet puts rhythm to work, however. To discuss all the ways in which rhythm can affect poetry would

fill an entire volume. The three methods covered here are meant to pro-
mote further investigation of meter. To help us delve into metrics, a
working vocabulary of metrical terms follows.

METRICAL VOCABULARY

foot: a unit of two or more syllables
   iambic foot: an unaccented syllable followed by an accented syllable (⌣/)
   trochaic foot: an accented syllable followed by an unaccented syllable (/⌣)
   dactylic foot: an accented syllable followed by two unaccented syllables (/⌣⌣)
   anapestic foot: two unaccented syllables followed by an accented syllable
   (⌣⌣/)
   spondaic foot: two accented syllables (//)
   pyrrhic foot: two unaccented syllables (⌣⌣)
   amphibrach: an unaccented syllable followed by an accented syllable and then
   by an unaccented syllable (⌣/⌣)

Meter: a rhythmical pattern

   monometer: one foot to the line (On a líne)

   dimeter: two feet to a line (Tóo sóon!/ Tóo sóon!)

   trimeter: three feet to a line (Míssing/ so múch/ and so múch)

   tetrameter: four feet to a line (Pícture your/self in a/boat on a/ ríver)

   pentameter: five feet to a line (He would/ adóre/ my gifts/ in stéad/ of mé)

   hexameter: six feet to a line (That líke/ a woun/ded snáke/ drags íts/ slów
   léngth/ alóng)

   Alexandrine: a hexameter line in which all feet are iambic (As óne/ for
   knight/ly giústs/ and fiérce/ encoún/ters fítt.)

   heptameter: seven feet to a line (O, rést/ ye, broth/er mar/íners,/ we wíll/
   not wán/der móre)

   octameter: eight feet to a line (When the/ lilac/scént was/ in the/ air and/
   Fifth-mónth/ gráss was/ grówing)

line (verse): a number of metrical feet that are usually, but not always, arranged
   to set up a pattern of expectations in the reader
   blank verse: unrhymed iambic pentameter
   free verse: nonmetrical or irregularly metrical lines
   enjambment (run-on line): a line carrying no punctuation at its end
   end-stopped line: a line carrying punctuation at its end
   caesura: a pause within a line

stanza: a grouping of two or more lines
couplet: two lines of verse with similar end-rhymes

> Nature and Nature's laws lay hid in *night*:
> God said, "Let Newton be!" and all was *light*.

tercet: three lines of verse rhyming *a a a* followed by three lines rhyming *b b b*

THE EAGLE

ALFRED, LORD TENNYSON

He clasps the crag with crooked hands;	*a*
Close to the sun in lonely lands,	*a*
Ringed with the azure world, he stands.	*a*
The wrinkled sea beneath him crawls;	*b*
He watches from his mountain walls,	*b*
And like a thunderbolt he falls.	*b*

quatrain: four lines of verse with a fixed pattern of rhyme and meter

He turned his face unto the wall,	*a*
And death with him was dealin':	*b*
"Adieu, adieu, my dear friends all,	*a*
And be kind to Barbara Allan."	*b*

rime royal: seven lines of iambic pentameter rhyming *a b a b b c c*

from THE RAPE OF LUCRECE

WILLIAM SHAKESPEARE

Those that much covet are with gain so fond,	*a*
For what they have not, that which they possess	*b*
They scatter and unloose it from their bond,	*a*
And so, by hoping more, they have but less;	*b*
Or, gaining more, the profit of excess	*b*
Is but to surfeit, and such griefs sustain,	*c*
That they prove bankrupt in this poor-rich gain.	*c*

ottava rima: eight lines of iambic pentameter rhyming *a b a b a b c c*

from DON JUAN

GEORGE GORDON, LORD BYRON

Under the bed they search'd, and there they found—	*a*
No matter what—it was not that they sought;	*b*
They open'd windows, gazing if the ground	*a*
Had signs or foot marks, but the earth said nought;	*b*
And then they stared each other's faces round:	*a*
'Tis odd, not one of all these seekers thought,	*b*
And seems to me almost a sort of blunder,	*c*
Of looking *in* the bed as well as under.	*c*

Spenserian stanza: eight lines of iambic pentameter followed by an Alexandrine and rhyming *a b a b b c b c c*

from THE EVE OF SAINT AGNES

JOHN KEATS

Full on this casement shone the wintry moon,	*a*
And threw warm gules on Madeline's fair breast,	*b*
As down she knelt for heaven's grace and boon;	*a*
Rose-bloom fell on her hands, together prest,	*b*
And on her silver cross soft amethyst,	*b*
And on her hair a glory, like a saint:	*c*
She seem'd a splendid angel, newly drest,	*b*
Save wings, for heaven:—Porphyro grew faint:	*c*
She knelt, so pure a thing, so free from mortal taint.	*c*

9
Man and Death

ONE STEP, AFTER STEP

GEORGE LANGSTON

One step, after step,
after step, only to reach
the last of the steps.

Death the unfathomable mystery, Death the shadowy figure wearing a cowled black robe, Death the fearful coachman, Death the merciful deliverer, Death the doorstep to immortality. Man has always regarded death with great awe, and he continues to do so today. Although most other mysteries of life have been or soon will be explained, death still puzzles man. "What *exactly* is death?" he continues to ask. With the advent of vital organ transplants, the important physical, ethical, and moral question, "When is one truly dead?" discomfits man more than ever.

The poems in this chapter deal with attitudes toward death. At times the speaker feels he has discovered the essence of death, as in Williams's "Death." Or he ponders a living death, as in Bill Miller's "On Being Nothing." At times Death is viewed in his old guise as the great leveler, as in "On Seeing a Hair of Lucretia Borgia." Sometimes death is the provoker of grief, as in "The Little One." Or death points an accusing finger at society, as in Dylan's "Who Killed Davey Moore?"

Each of the following six poems deals with the discovery of death. Considering central purpose, meter, structure, diction, imagery, figurative language, and tone, compare and contrast them with one another.

UNTITLED

SHARON BUCK

I'M DEAD.
The sun is pink
and yellow lost its life
last night
into a moon   5
eons away
unreachable.
I reached.

Pink—diluted blood.
hazy hearts   10
eons away.
I never reached
they say.
Hard to say.

DEATH

WILLIAM CARLOS WILLIAMS

So this is death that I
refuse to rouse and write
but prefer to lie here
half asleep with a mind

not aflame but merely   5
flickering lacking breath
to fan it—from
the comfortable dark womb

OBIT

DANIEL BERRIGAN

We die perplexed, dwarfed by the petty
crises we thought contained, controlled

showing like frayed pockets, space within
without, for loss.
                    Pain in eyes, a ragged   5
animal before the gun;
                    muzzily—
can death do any harm
life hasn't done? maybe
                    dreamily *death*   10
turns old dogs
into fish hillsides butterflies
                    teaches a new
trick or two

COLLOQUY

JOHN HALL WHEELOCK

"It isn't fair. It isn't fair.
What's the good of being dead
If you won't know that you are?" he said.

"You silly ass, to give a care!
You won't be there, you'll be everywhere,   5
And somebody else'll be there instead."

DEATH

DANIEL BERRIGAN

He was on stilts
fifty miles high
with a big paper
sunflower for eye
said with a grin   5
taking me in his arms
well
Horatio
how do things look
from up here?   10

ON BEING NOTHING

BILL MILLER

The day I leaped into my mind
And never did touch down,
Is the day I discovered the floating death,
The floating live-death, of being nothing.
And as I drift through the void,   5
I recognize the folly of withdrawal,
Of being nowhere, being nothing,
When life is somewhere, being something.
I feel (and that's something)
I'd rather have death, than no life,   10
Than the floating death,
Than the floating live-death
Of being nothing.

ON SEEING A HAIR OF LUCRETIA BORGIA

WALTER SAVAGE LANDOR

Borgia, thou once wert almost too august
And high for adoration—now thou'rt dust;
All that remains of thee these plaits infold,
Calm hair, meandering with pellucid gold!

Define *august* and *pellucid.*
Lucretia Borgia was duchess of Ferrara, 1480–1519, and a patroness
of the arts. What does this poem suggest about her?
What is the central purpose of the poem?

THE FUNERAL

JOHN DONNE

Whoever comes to shroud me, do not harm
    Nor question much
That subtle wreath of hair which crowns my arm;
The mystery, the sign you must not touch,

147

For 'tis my outward soul,   5
Viceroy to that, which then to heaven being gone,
  Will leave this to control,
And keep these limbs, her provinces, from dissolution.

For if the sinewy thread my brain lets fall
  Through every part   10
Can tie those parts and make me one of all;
These hairs, which upward grew, and strength and art
  Have from a better brain,
Can better do it; except she meant that I
  By this should know my pain,   15
As prisoners then are manacled, when they're condemned to die.

Whate'er she meant by it, bury it with me,
  For since I am
Love's martyr, it might breed idolatry,
If into others' hands these relics came;   20
  As 'twas humility
To afford to it all that a soul can do,
  So 'tis some bravery,
That since you would save none of me, I bury some of you.

The speaker talks about a lock of his lady's hair that he wears on his
arm. Why does he wear it? Does he view the lock as it was originally
indended to be viewed? From where does he speak? What has happened
to him? How does he feel about it?
What is the tone of the poem?

ELEGY

THEODORE ROETHKE

Her face like a rain-beaten stone on the day she rolled off
With the dark hearse, and enough flowers for an alderman,—
And so she was, in her way, Aunt Tilly.

Sighs, sighs, who says they have sequence?
Between the spirit and the flesh,—what war?   5
She never knew;
For she asked no quarter and gave none,
Who sat with the dead when the relatives left,

Who fed and tended the infirm, the mad, the epileptic,
And, with a harsh rasp of a laugh at herself,   10
Faced up to the worst.

I recall how she harried the children away all the late summer
From the one beautiful thing in her yard, the peachtree;
How she kept the wizened, the fallen, the misshapen for herself,
And picked and pickled the best, to be left on rickety doorsteps.   15
And yet she died in agony,
Her tongue, at the last, thick, black as an ox's.

Terror of cops, bill collectors, betrayers of the poor,—
I see you in some celestial supermarket,
Moving serenely among the leeks and cabbages,   20
Probing the squash,
Bearing down, with two steady eyes,
On the quaking butcher.

What kind of person was Aunt Tilly? How do we know?

How does the speaker feel about her death? From what can we infer this?

What metrical form does this poem take? How does the form affect the central idea?

What is the tone?

AUNT HELEN

T. S. ELIOT

Miss Helen Slingsby was my maiden aunt,
And lived in a small house near a fashionable square
Cared for by servants to the number of four.
Now when she died there was silence in heaven
And silence at her end of the street.   5
The shutters were drawn and the undertaker wiped his feet—
He was aware that this sort of thing had occurred before.
The dogs were handsomely provided for,
But shortly afterwards the parrot died too.
The Dresden clock continued ticking on the mantelpiece,   10
And the footman sat upon the dining-table
Holding the second housemaid on his knees—
Who had always been so careful while her mistress lived.

What can we infer about Aunt Helen? What specific things indicate
this? Compare Aunt Helen to Aunt Tilly of "Elegy."
What do the silence, the drawn shutters, the undertaker wiping his feet
suggest? Is there perhaps *ambiguity* (multiple meaning) in this poem?
What do the provisions made for the pets suggest?
What do the actions of the servants suggest?

NOT FORGOTTEN .2. DREAM

PETER DAVISON

I stood alone at a funeral. It was up to me
To pronounce the oration. My tongue was knotted fast,
And every mourner rolled his maggot eyes.
The reek of greenhouse flowers pressed on ears
Still filled with Handel's "Largo," while the bright box   5
Gleamed like a conference table proof against speeches.
Toward the rear of the chapel, twisting kleenex,
Sat ranks of visitors, urged to stop in on their way
To another appointment by friends who had assured them
This would not take long. It was taking longer and longer.   10

Who was dead? It was up to me to remember.
I had ransacked my pockets twice—no memoranda—
And my Oxford Book of Consolations had vanished.
The penguin crowd creaked folding chairs impatiently,
So with nothing at all to say, I did what I did: 15
Danced a very respectful dance on the coffin.
The guest of honor drummed her cold toes
On the underside of the lid.

Consider the language of this poem. What are "maggot eyes"? How
can flowers "press on ears"? Why a "penguin crowd"? What does the
speaker mean when he says that he "danced" on the coffin? What can be
inferred from lines five through ten?
Who is the speaker? How does he feel about the funeral?
Interpret the last two lines.

THE LITTLE ONE

JOHN CIARDI

And if you do not weep,
at what are you used to weeping?
—UGOLINO

The little one
chilled paler and paler   5
till the smile in her
wisped off
like breath in a frost.

Then, last, her eyes went out.
By that nightfall   10
the snow on the sill
had let out glass claws,
and what man was not scratched
could have no tears in this world
nor hope of dear smiling.   15

All our silences walked those rooms,
walked us,
tore and took
what we did not say.

"This is what Nothing is,"   20
said our silences.
"And this," said the winter mounds
that had to be blasted open
even for so little a one
to slide into   25
            to Nothing.

The epigraph of this poem is taken from Dante's *Inferno*. Ugolino has been telling Dante how he and his four young sons were starved to death in a walled prison, how the boys died one by one while he stood helplessly by. What does this allusion contribute to the poem?

What image patterns do you find? How do they contribute to the total poem?

What figures of speech do you find? Note particularly lines eight, nine, and twelve.

Compare the tone of this poem to the tone of "Not Forgotten."

FATHER'S FACE

ALFRED K. WEBER

Even tears of grief
work their fragile lines
into the rock and
with time those signs
shape a relief.   5

In what senses is the word *relief* used?
What is the speaker saying about grief?

THE TAG

BERT ALMON

My father's dog tag lying in a drawer
The name misspelled, the date correct.
A disc struck off, like me in wartime
A time of tending buoys and driving trucks
Of slipping off to sleep in his own bed   5
With his new wife in a roach-filled room.

I rub the metal of my inheritance
Its letters worn smooth by years on a chain
Years that began before my memories.
Those days shut tight to recollection   10
Will open a little to hearsay and snapshots:

The fragments of a man's life in a drawer
For another tag of his existence
To hold in hand and read correctly.

In what senses is the word *tag* used? What do these senses of the word
imply?

What can be inferred from the misspelled name on the dog tag? How
does this fact relate to the final line?

ELEGY V

AUGUSTINE BOWE

I do not laugh at all of the nice things:
At the bronze coffin, the gathered flowers,
Nor at the way the lurid contralto sings,
Not at you and the rest of your wasted hours.

This was a nice funeral, my wife was sad;   5
My children wept their eyes out and the preacher
Said a mouthful. "It was too bad,"
(As she put her arm around my child) said the teacher.

The Legion did its bit and shot a volley
After the ritual at my grave.   10
My wife seemed to enjoy their noisy folly;
They gave her the empty shells to save.

What can be inferred from the diction? Note particularly the words
nice and *mouthful* in stanza II and *folly* and *empty* of stanza III.
What is a "lurid" contralto?
What is the significance of the empty shells?
Comment on the meter and stanzaic pattern. How do they affect the
central purpose?
What comment does the poem make about death?
What is the tone?

AFTER DEATH

CHRISTINA ROSSETTI

The curtains were half drawn; the floor was swept
    And strewn with rushes; rosemary and may
    Lay thick upon the bed on which I lay,
Where, through the lattice, ivy-shadows crept.
He leaned above me, thinking that I slept   5
    And could not hear him; but I heard him say,
    "Poor child, poor child"; and as he turned away
Came a deep silence, and I knew he wept.
He did not touch the shroud, or raise the fold

That hid my face, or take my hand in his,   10
Or ruffle the smooth pillows for my head.
He did not love me living; but once dead
He pitied me; and very sweet it is
To know he still is warm though I am cold.

Who is the speaker? What kind of person is she? How do we know?
What is the situation?
Interpret the last three lines. What is their tone? Can you reconcile it
with the tone of the rest of the poem?
Compare "After Death" to John Donne's "Funeral."

WHO KILLED DAVEY MOORE?

BOB DYLAN

Who killed Davey Moore,
Why an' what's the reason for?
"Not I," says the referee,
"Don't point your finger at me.
I could've stopped it in the eighth   5
An' maybe kept him from his fate,
But the crowd would've booed I'm sure
At not gettin' their money's worth.
It's too bad he had to go
But there was pressure on me too, you know.   10
It wasn't me that made him fall,
No you can't blame me at all."

"Not us," says the angry crowd,
Whose screams filled the arena loud.
"It's too bad he died that nite   15
But we just like to see a fight.
We didn't mean for him t' meet his death
We just meant to see some sweat,
There ain't nothin' wrong in that.
It wasn't us that made him fall   20
No you can't blame us at all."

"Not me," says his manager,
Puffing on a big cigar,
"It's hard to say, it's hard to tell
I always thought that he was well.   25
It's too bad for his wife an' kids he's dead,

But if he was sick, he should've said.
It wasn't me that made him fall
No you can't blame me at all."

"Not me," says the gambling man,   30
With his ticket stub still in his hand,
"It wasn't me that knocked him down
My hands never touched him none.
I didn't commit no ugly sin,
Anyway I put money on him to win.   35
It wasn't me that made him fall
No you can't blame me at all."

"Not me," says the boxing writer,
Pounding print on his old typewriter,
Sayin' "boxing ain't to blame   40
There's just as much danger in a football game."
Sayin' "fist fighting is here to stay
It's just the old American way.
It wasn't me that made him fall
No you can't blame me at all."   45

"Not me," says the man whose fists
Laid him low in a cloud of mist,
Who came here from Cuba's door
Where boxing ain't allowed no more.   45
"I hit him, yes, it's true,
But that's what I am paid to do.
Don't say 'murder,' don't say 'kill,'
It was destiny, it was God's will."

Who is Davey Moore? What does he represent in this poem?
Characterize the people who disclaim responsibility for his death.
Is the lyric a comment on death or a comment on society?

ABC OF CULTURE

HARVEY SHAPIRO

So the angel of death whistles Mozart
(As we knew he would)
Bicycling amid the smoke of Auschwitz,
The Jews of Auschwitz,
In the great museum of Western Art.   5

Man and Death

Why should the angel of death whistle Mozart?
What does the image of this bicycling angel suggest?
How does the title relate to the poem?
In what sense are we to take the final line?

THE REBEL

When I
die
I'm sure
I will have a
Big Funeral . . .   5
Curiosity
seekers . . .
coming to see
if I
am really   10
Dead . . .
or just
trying to make
Trouble. . . .

MUSÉE DES BEAUX ARTS

About suffering they were never wrong,
The Old Masters: how well they understood
Its human position; how it takes place
While someone else is eating or opening a window or
    just walking dully along;
How, when the aged are reverently, passionately waiting   5
For the miraculous birth, there always must be
Children who did not specially want it to happen, skating
On a pond at the edge of the wood:
They never forgot
That even the dreadful martyrdom must run its course   10
Anyhow in a corner, some untidy spot
Where the dogs go on with their doggy life and the
    torturer's horse
Scratches its innocent behind on a tree.

In Brueghel's *Icarus*, for instance: how everything turns
  away
Quite leisurely from the disaster; the plowman may   15
Have heard the splash, the forsaken cry,
But for him it was not an important failure; the sun shone
As it had to on the white legs disappearing into the green
Water; and the expensive delicate ship that must have seen
Something amazing, a boy falling out of the sky,   20
Had somewhere to get to and sailed calmly on.

The title of this poem refers to a famous art museum in Brussels where a painting by Brueghel depicting the fall of Icarus hangs. According to the myth, Icarus and his father, Daedalus, to escape from an island prison, built wings of wax and feathers. Disregarding his father's warning, Icarus flew too close to the sun and fell to his death. How do the myth and its depiction by Brueghel contribute to the theme of the poem?
What is the "it" being talked about in the poem?
What is the "miraculous birth"?
What do the skating children add to the poem?
What do the dogs and horse suggests?

THE IMMIGRANT'S WAKE AND REQUIEM

REUEL DENNEY

Five Irish waiters all looking like St. Anthony,
With aprons from Ruppert's and black suits from Goldberg's,
Marched across the river and they marched across the ferry
And marched along the Avenue, four with coffin poles.
In the March wind their aprons stood up with the starching.   5
Their black hair was blown. Their chins were all heavy.
Their jaws needed shaving. They did not look happy.
They carried the coffin of O'Hodhead the fireman.
Yet they laughed with the corpse and their manner was merry
When they coffied at Luchow's. They rested for whiskey   10
At Cassidy's Oysters. They smiled as the red-head
Swung her butt as they passed and made on for St. Patrick's.
They hummed in Gregorian, musical hodmen.
They were joined as they marched by a friar from Fordham
Who carried a handkerchief. This cousin was learned   15
And seemed like a Spaniard; he recorded his culpas
And kept memoes on footnotes and signals for football
On rosaries of knuckles from the pigs killed at Cudahy's.

Who knows what they thought, the five pious bearers
Who marched there so well and so rugged and so chilly?   20
But my, what a sight they made, marching and flapping
The black of their coats and the white of their napery
Hired just pressed, with respect to the services!
Into the church they went, praise them, the carriers,
Thinking their best, not their last, of that traveller.   25

Describe the waiters. How does the setting help to define them? How does their mission also help?
What is the tone of this poem? What specific things contribute to it?

DIES IRAE

AUGUSTINE BOWE

Black velvet hangs on the cathedral walls.
The organ, death-struck, is wailing.
They read the office in the sanctuary stalls,
The beggars kneel at the iron paling.
The hearse must be back in town by three.   5
There is an hour for death, an hour for tea.
Hostlers must curry the mournful mare;
Oats do better than graveyard air
To polish her black and glossy sadness—
Than all this plush Gregorian madness.   10

Comment on the diction. What is "Gregorian madness"?
What images are evoked? What do they suggest?
What do all of the things that "must" be done suggest?

from HOMAGE TO QUINTUS SEPTIMIUS
FLORENTIS CHRISTIANUS

EZRA POUND

A sad and great evil is the expectation of death—
And there are also the inane expenses of the funeral;
Let us therefore cease from pitying the dead
For after death there comes no other calamity.

10
Poetry
and Melody

The title of this chapter may seem strange to you at first. "Poetry consists of an arrangement of words," you may say. "Without notes or musical instruments, how can it possibly be melodic?" Think back to Chapter 8 for a moment, though. There we saw that poetry, like music, has rhythm. But rhythm alone would be insufficient evidence on which to base a chapter on "Poetry and Melody." We are talking now not only about rhythm, but also about the sound patterns of poetry.

Sound patterns are closely related to the other tools of the poet. By nature, sound patterns emanate directly from the words and their rhythm. The skillful poet may choose and arrange his words as much for the resulting sound patterns as for meaning. He often manipulates sound as he manipulates meter, to emphasize and to imitate his meaning and his subject. A few poets write abstract poetry which, like abstract painting in which meaning is conveyed by shapes and colors rather than by representation of actual objects, relies chiefly on sound patterns and sound qualities to convey meaning.

JABBERWOCKY

LEWIS CARROLL

'Twas brillig, and the slithy toves
    Did gyre and gimble in the wabe;
All mimsy were the borogoves,
    And the mome raths outgrabe.

"Beware the Jabberwock, my son!   5
    The jaws that bite, the claws that catch!
Beware the Jubjub bird, and shun
    The frumious Bandersnatch!"

He took his vorpal sword in hand;
    Long time the manxome foe he sought—   10
So rested he by the Tumtum tree,
    And stood awhile in thought.

And, as in uffish thought he stood,
    The Jabberwock, with eyes of flame,
Came whiffling through the tulgey wood,   15
    And burbled as it came!

One, two! One, two! And through and through
    The vorpal blade went snicker-snack!
He left it dead, and with its head
    He went galumphing back.   20

"And hast thou slain the Jabberwock?
    Come to my arms, my beamish boy!
O frabjous day! Callooh! Callay!"
    He chortled in his joy.

'Twas brillig, and the slithy toves   25
    Did gyre and gimble in the wabe;
All mimsy were the borogoves,
    And the mome raths outgrabe.

Carroll's diction is pure nonsense, but he seems to make some sense because he follows normal English word construction, *syntax* (word order), and sound patterns with his nonsense words. Most poets, hovever, do not use sound as obviously as Carroll.

One of the masters of poetic sound manipulation was Wallace Stevens:

PETER QUINCE AT THE CLAVIER

WALLACE STEVENS

I

Just as my fingers on these keys
Make music, so the selfsame sounds
On my spirit make a music, too.

Music is feeling, then, not sound;
And thus it is that what I feel,   5
Here in this room, desiring you,

Thinking of your blue-shadowed silk,
Is music. It is like the strain
Waked in the elders by Susanna.

Of a green evening, clear and warm,   10
She bathed in her still garden, while
The red-eyed elders watching, felt

The basses of their beings throb
In witching chords, and their thin blood
Pulse pizzicatti of Hosanna.   15

II

In the green water, clear and warm,
Susanna lay.
She searched
The touch of springs,
And found   20
Concealed imaginings.
She sighed,
For so much melody.

Upon the bank, she stood
In the cool   25
Of spent emotions.
She felt, among the leaves,
The dew
Of old devotions.

She walked upon the grass,   30
Still quavering.
The winds were like her maids,
On timid feet,
Fetching her woven scarves,
Yet wavering.   35

A breath upon her hand
Muted the night.
She turned—
A cymbal crashed,
And rearing horns.   40

III

Soon, with a noise like tambourines,
Came her attendant Byzantines.

They wondered why Susanna cried
Against the elders by her side;

And as they whispered, the refrain   45
Was like a willow swept by rain.

Anon, their lamps' uplifted flame
Revealed Susanna and her shame.

And then, the simpering Byzantines
Fled, with a noise like tambourines.   50

IV

Beauty is momentary in the mind—
The fitful tracing of a portal;
But in the flesh it is immortal.

The body dies; the body's beauty lives.
So evenings die, in their green going,   55
A wave, interminably flowing.
So gardens die, their meek breath scenting
The cowl of winter, done repenting.
So maidens die, to the auroral
Celebration of a maiden's choral.   60

Susanna's music touched the bawdy strings
Of those white elders; but, escaping,
Left only Death's ironic scraping.
Now, in its immortality, it plays
On the clear viol of her memory,   65
And makes a constant sacrament of praise.

Peter Quince was a character in Shakespeare's *Midsummer Night's Dream*. He was carpenter and stage manager for a play within the play, "Pyramus and Thisbe." In other words, he was both a creator and a manipulator, just as he is in Stevens's poem as he sits at the clavier (a musical instrument resembling a piano), both creating the music he plays and manipulating it and the tale around which his composition is built. In the tale, "Susanna and the Elders" from the *King James Apocrypha,* Susanna was falsely accused by two elders of unchastity because she refused their amorous advances when they found her bathing alone. After causing Susanna much anguish, the elders were later exposed by Daniel through separate questioning and put to death. Although knowing this allusion helps us understand the poem, the sound patterns are also extremely important. The four sections of the poem, each unique in sound, together build the total poem like a musical composition:

> Just as my fingers on these keys
> Make music, so the selfsame sounds
> On my spirit make a music, too.
>
> Music is feeling, then, not sound;
> And thus it is that what I feel,
> Here in this room, desiring you,
>
> Thinking of your blue-shadowed silk,
> Is music.

The musician compares his amorous desire to music, a comparison he expands even further by alluding to the story of Susanna. Note how in these first few lines (which are basically iambic tetrameter) the initial trochaic foot of each line sets up a kind of musical beat within the lines. Also notice that the music here is the relatively quiet, exploratory sound made by a pianist beginning a composition. The quiet mood is maintained by the regular meter, to be sure, but more important to maintaining the mood are the sound patterns set up by *alliteration* (the repetition of initial, identical consonant sounds or any vowel sounds that are closely associated or immediately following one another) of the twanging nasals *m* and *n*, the hissing *s*'s and the flowing liquids *l* and *r*. As the first part of the poem ends, however, a change occurs:

> . . . It is like the strain   /
> Waked in the elders by Susanna.
>
> Of a green evening, clear and warm,
> She bathed in her still garden, while
> The red-eyed elders watching, felt
>
> The basses of their beings throb
> In witching chords, and their thin blood
> Pulse pizzicatti of Hosanna.

The mellifluous music of the early lines is disrupted by the growing undercurrent of throbbing *b*'s, *p*'s, and *d*'s which introduce the "pizzicatti" and "basses" of the changing music that accompanies the mention of the lecherous elders. This music will be picked up once again in part III, where the elders intrude on Susanna's pristine solitude. The first part of the poem, then, sets up not only the subject of the poem (the musician's desire) and the manner in which this subject will be developed (through allusion both to the story of Susanna and to music), but also themes from the prevailing "music" of the entire poem. As part I ends in hints of pizzicatti and basses, another shift in music occurs.

Part II, which deals with Susanna herself, has another mood:

> In the green water, clear and warm,
> Susanna lay.
> She searched
> The touch of springs,
> And found
> Concealed imaginings.
> She sighed,
> For so much melody.
>
> Upon the bank, she stood
> In the cool
> Of spent emotions.
> She felt, among the leaves,
> The dew
> Of old devotions.
>
> She walked upon the grass,
> Still quavering.
> The winds were like her maids,
> On timid feet,
> Fetching her woven scarves,
> Yet wavering.

Like Susanna standing on the grass, and like her maids, the music of this section is wispy and tenuous. The initial pyrrhic foot, followed by irregular meter throughout; the *triple rime* (three consecutive syllables with corresponding sounds) of lines eleven fourteen, sixteen, and twenty ("emotions," "devotions," "quavering," and "wavering"); and the lightly hissing *s*'s, resonant *w*'s, and softly twanging *m*'s and *ng*'s cause the sound patterns to quaver and waver like Susanna. But the diaphanous dance step is soon disrupted by another shift in the music as the section depicting Susanna's delicacy gives way to one that describes the utter grossness of the elders:

> A breath upon her hand
> Muted the night.

> She turned—
> A cymbal crashed,
> And rearing horns.

The reader is prepared for and led into part III with the entrance of the lecherous and lying elders heralded by the discordant crash of cymbals and brass, a fanfare for the rattle of tambourines at the beginning of part III:

> Soon, with a noise like tambourines,
> Came her attendant Byzantines.
>
> They wondered why Susanna cried
> Against the elders by her side;
>
> And as they whispered, the refrain
> Was like a willow swept by rain.
>
> Anon, their lamps' uplifted flame
> Revealed Susanna and her shame.
>
> And then, the simpering Byzantines
> Fled, with a noise like tambourines.

The complete regularity of these lines—the closed *couplets* (verses having two lines with rhymes occurring at the ends of the lines), and the unbroken iambic tetrameter—contrasts strongly with the light, almost flippant irregularity of the preceding movement of the poem. The strict, almost militaristic beat echoes the deliberately insistent intensity of the tambourines intruding into the melody, and the deliberately throbbing lechery and lies of the elders, causing the Byzantines to turn blindly against Susanna.

The final section of the poem blends all the previously mentioned musical effects into a fugue-like finale:

> Beauty is momentary in the mind—
> The fitful tracing of a portal;
> But in the flesh it is immortal.
>
> The body dies; the body's beauty lives.
> So evenings die, in their green going,
> A wave, interminably flowing.
>
> So gardens die, their meek breath scenting
> The cowl of winter, done repenting.

So maidens die, to the auroral
Celebration of a maiden's choral.

Susanna's music touched the bawdy strings
Of those white elders; but, escaping,
Left only Death's ironic scraping.
Now, in its immortality, it plays
On the clear viol of her memory,
And makes a constant sacrament of praise.

In this section the reechoing end-rhymes of the tambourine section blend with the haunting dance of part II in *feminine rime* (a rhyme, sometimes called *double rime,* falling on two syllables, the first accented and the second unaccented):

So gardens die, their meek breath scenting
The cowl of winter, done repenting.

These lines also contain the harsh, throbbing *b*'s *p*'s *d*'s, and *g*'s that introduced the lecherous elders and the soft, twanging *m*'s and *n*'s of the quiet music of part I. The poem, then, presents four definite sound patterns, modeled on the movements of a musical score, that echo the poem's narrative and subject.

Stevens plays with the sounds of music in another poem, "The Man with the Blue Guitar," part of which follows. Alluding to a Picasso painting, Stevens pursues a perennial and somewhat slippery theme: the artist's relationship to reality. He pursues this theme verse after verse and stanza after stanza in a dialogue between a somewhat ambiguous "they" and the artist, who creates upon his blue guitar. The dialogue continuously and ultimately circles back to the beginning statements:

They said, "You have a blue guitar,
You do not play things as they are."

The man replied, "Things as they are
Are changed upon the blue guitar."

Reality ("things as they are") changes in one's imagination (represented by the blue guitar). The man with the guitar is, we are told, "a shears-man of sorts": he pares objective reality to a new kind of reality—art— which emerges from his blue guitar. He is the poet who attempts to capture upon the page the essence of reality; and he ultimately finds that "things as they are" cannot be transferred intact from their natural state

into a newly created state. Change is imperative. Just as change is impera-
tive in the creative process, so each attempt to recreate brings further
change. This series of changes is the subject of the thirty-three stanzas of
the poem. As the poem progresses—and at times regresses—we can follow
several shifts.

The most obvious shift is the alternation between speakers. The mys-
terious "they" speaks for one, two, or three stanzas and are followed by
rebuttal from the guitarist or his guitar. "They" ask the guitarist to play
"a tune upon the blue guitar/of things exactly as they are." Note that
the plurality of the speaker echoes the plurality of "things as they are."
In fact, this very plurality may make it impossible for the artist to cap-
ture total reality. Because we all see things differently, the guitarist must
answer that he can only "sing a hero's head . . . but not a man." Metri-
cally and melodically the dilemma is echoed when the guitarist begins to
plunk his instrument:

> To strike his living hi and ho,
> To tick it, tock it, turn it true,
>
> To bang it from a savage blue,
> Jangling the metal of the strings . . .

Although the basic metrical pattern (iambic tetrameter) is maintained,
the jarring alliteration (the numerous *t*'s, for example) parallels the jar-
ring of reality when the guitarist attempts to recreate it on his guitar. Fur-
thermore, the final ellipses of the stanza suggest the ultimate defeat of
the artist's attempt.

The guitarist makes numerous attempts to capture "things as they
are," with slight variations. In stanza IV the guitar "buzz[es]," in stanza
V it "chatter[s]," and by stanza VIII it sounds with a "leaden twang."
Notice how these *onomatopoeic* words (words whose sounds echo their
sense) carry melodic effects.

Just as his music does not always blend, the guitarist finds it impos-
sible to fuse reality and imagination into the same entity:

> A few final solutions, like a duet
> With the undertaker: a voice in the clouds,
>
> Another on earth, the one a voice
> Of ether, the other smelling of drink,
>
> The voice of ether prevailing, the swell
> Of the undertaker's song in the snow

Apostrophizing wreaths, the voice
In the clouds serene and final, next

The grunted breath serene and final,
The imagined and the real, thought

And the truth, Dichtung and Wahrheit, all
Confusion solved, as in a refrain

One keeps on playing year by year,
Concerning the nature of things as they are.

In other words, reality and imagination sing as a duet, but each has a different voice. With "all/ Confusion solved," then, the guitarist begins to play his guitar in earnest, no longer trying to force from it "things as they are":

He held the world upon his nose
And this-a-way he gave a fling.

His robes and symbols, ai-yi-yi—
And that-a-way he twirled the thing.

Sombre as fir-trees, liquid cats
Moved in the grass without a sound.

They did not know the grass went round.
The cats had cats and the grass turned gray

And the world had worlds, ai, this-a-way:
The grass turned green and the grass turned gray.

And the nose is eternal, that-a-way.
Things as they were, things as they are,

Things as they will be by and by . . .
A fat thumb beats out ai-yi-yi.

Reality is changed into whatever the guitarist or artist desires. Things as they are are turned this-a-way and that-a-way: cats may be liquid, and grass both gray and green according to the whim of the artist. We need only read the poem aloud to hear that the earlier jarring sounds of the guitar have changed to smooth, sure, free, and resounding music. Although the meter remains the iambic tetrameter of the beginning, the effect is totally different. The movement is no longer slowed or stilted by grating alliteration, as in the beginning. Here we can both hear and feel the rousing music of the singing guitar, and it matters little whether the words seem nonsensical because, like the guitarist, the reader has accepted the premise that things will not be "as they are" when they have been recreated on the blue guitar. We could almost dance to the flying flamenco music of these lines. The melodic effect is enhanced by long vowels used profusely throughout the passage, by recurring end-rhymes, by combinations of *th* and *s* and *g*, *b*, and *c*, and by the recurring refrains "this-a-way," "that-a-way," and "ai-yi-yi." This particular passage sings more melodically perhaps than any other passage written and is an excellent one in which to hear the music of poetry.

Our examination of the melody of these poems is meant only to suggest how we might look at other poems to heighten our understanding and enjoyment of poetry. Technical vocabulary has been kept to a minimum in our discussion; additional vocabulary that may be useful should we wish to discuss sound patterns of other poems in more detail follows.

Vocabulary

euphony: a pleasant sound created by certain combinations of words

cacophony: harsh and unpleasant sounds created by certain combinations of words

onomatopoeia: reflection of the meaning of words in their sound (*buzz, clink, clank, oink, rattle, gurgle*)

rhyme: similar or identical sounds in two or more syllables

    end-rime: rhyme that occurs at the end of lines

> Struggling in my father's *hands,*
> Striving against my swaddling *bands,*

    internal rhyme (Leonine rhyme): rhyme that occurs somewhere between the beginning and closing syllables of the verse

> And Tib my *wife,* that as her *life*
> Loveth well good ale to seek,
> Full oft drinks *she,* till ye may *see*
> The tears run down her cheeks.

    masculine rhyme: rhyme that occurs only in the final syllables of lines

> Honor thy parents; that is, *all*
> From whom advancement may be*fall.*

    feminine rhyme (double rhyme): rhyme that occurs on two consecutive syllables

Soon break, soon wither, soon for*gotten*—
In folly ripe, in reason *rotten*.

triple rhyme: rhyme that occurs on three consecutive syllables

Take her up *tenderly*,
Lift her with care;
Fashion'd so *slenderly*,
Young, and so fair!

slant rhyme: rhyme that is approximate

He sent his man down through the town
To the place where she was *dwellin'*:
"O haste and come to my master dear,
Gin ye be Barbara *Allan*."

consonance: the final consonants in stressed syllables correspond in sound, but
the vowels preceding them do not (*bull–ball, jump–tramp*)
assonance: sound correspondence occurring on vowels followed by different
consonants (*plate–fake, tool–toot*)
alliteration: sound correspondence on initial consonants or on any vowel in
words closely following one another

Swiftly, swiftly flew the ship,
Yet she sailed softly too:
Sweetly, sweetly blew the breeze—
On me alone it blew.

Alone, alone, all, all alone,
Alone on a wide wide sea!
And never a saint took pity on
My soul in agony.

11
Man and the Gods

THE PROUD TREE TOSSES

FRANK MEZTA

The proud tree tosses
in the violent wind, but
who tosses the wind?

Throughout history man has worshiped some strange gods. Prehistoric man and modern aborigines bowed down to sticks and stones. Greeks and Romans built temples to capricious gods who possessed human shapes and foibles. Medieval man cherished sacred relics bought from devious traveling churchmen who raided trash piles for their wares (as Chaucer chronicled in *Canterbury Tales*). Bloody wars and inquisitions have been waged, even during the enlightened twentieth century, to identify and strike down worshipers of "false" gods. Recently, Western man has tended to turn away from traditional gods to worship either political systems (communism, for example) or more visible material things ("neon gods" and status symbols) or to seek revelation in the occult (astrology, tarot cards, black magic, or I-Ching, for example). It continues to be extremely difficult, if not impossible, to determine who worships the true God.

Most modern poets question the gods. Some question the validity of one kind of god or another, as Ciardi does in "Beagles." Some advocate complete hedonism, as FitzGerald does in "The Rubáiyát of Omar Khayyám." Some point out the absurdity of man's creation of an anthropomorphic God, as Browning does in "Caliban upon Setebos." And some look hopefully toward a new millennium for man's salvation, as Yeats does in "The Second Coming." The single common note, however, is one of uncertainty, questioning, searching for a much-needed Something beyond oneself and one's environment which can truly be labeled God.

BEAGLES

for Kenneth Rexroth

JOHN CIARDI

Beagles have big eyes and wet noses
and when they fall in love with any
part of humanity they stay there
as if it were important.

Had beagles as much sense as incest   5
in their pedigrees, they might learn maybe
to squint a little, and to wipe their noses,
when they look at what they take for God.

The speaker suggests that beagles worship false gods—men. Can anything beyond this be inferred from this poem? Why?

WHAT THE WITCH SAID

HARVEY SHAPIRO

I would not want to see
Gods ascending out of the earth
Or the dead living.
How can they talk so easily
Of a stone rolled   5
From the cave's mouth,
Of spirits crowding a ditch to drink?
What banquet
Draws them to the dead,
What tender eating?   10

To what events does this poem allude?
How important is the title?
How does the speaker feel about "what the witch said"?

from THE RUBÁIYÁT OF OMAR KHAYYÁM

EDWARD FITZGERALD

12

A Book of Verses underneath the Bough,   45
A Jug of Wine, a Loaf of Bread—and Thou
    Beside me singing in the Wilderness—
Oh, Wilderness were Paradise enow!

13

Some for the Glories of This World; and some
Sigh for the Prophet's Paradise to come;   50
    Ah, take the Cash, and let the Credit go,
Nor heed the rumble of a distant Drum!

24

Ah, make the most of what we yet may spend,
Before we too into the Dust descend;
    Dust into Dust, and under Dust to lie,   95
Sans Wine, sans Song, sans Singer, and—sans End!

Juxtaposed here are "Glories of This World" and "the Prophet's Para-
dise." Who is the Prophet? What is the distant Drum?

Comment on the speaker's faith. How does it compare with the faith
demonstrated in "Beagles"?

Notice the final line. What does the punctuation contribute to the
effect?

What is the tone of the poem?

from CALIBAN UPON SETEBOS

ROBERT BROWNING

'Thinketh, He made thereat the sun, this isle,
Trees and the fowls here, beast and creeping thing.   45
Yon otter, sleek-wet, black, lithe as a leech;
Yon auk, one fire-eye in a ball of foam,
That floats and feeds; a certain badger brown
He hath watched hunt with that slant white-wedge eye
By moonlight; and the pie[1] with the long tongue   50

---

[1] magpie

That pricks deep into oakwarts for a worm,
And says a plain word when she finds her prize,
But will not eat the ants; the ants themselves .
That build a wall of seeds and settled stalks
About their hole—He made all these and more,   55
Made all we see, and us, in spite: how else?
He could not, Himself, make a second self
To be His mate; as well have made Himself:
He would not make what He mislikes or slights,
An eyesore to Him, or not worth His pains: 60
But did, in envy, listlessness, or sport,
Make what Himself would fain, in a manner, be—
Weaker in most points, stronger in a few,
Worthy, and yet mere playthings all the while,
Things He admires and mocks too—that is it.   65
Because, so brave, so better though they be,
It nothing skills if He begin to plague.
Look now, I melt a gourd-fruit into mash,
Add honeycomb and pods, I have perceived,
Which bite like finches when they bill and kiss—   70
Then, when froth rises bladdery, drink up all,
Quick, quick, till maggots scamper through my brain;
Last, throw me on my back i' the seeded thyme,
And wanton, wishing I were born a bird.
Put case, unable to be what I wish,   75
I yet could make a live bird out of clay:
Would not I take clay, pinch my Caliban
Able to fly?—for, there, see, he hath wings,
And great comb like the hoopoe's[2] to admire,
And there, a sting to do his foes offense,   80
There, and I will that he begin to live,
Fly to yon rock-top, nip me off the horns
Of grigs high up that make the merry din,
Saucy through their veined wings, and mind me not.
In which feat, if his leg snapped, brittle clay,   85
And he lay stupid-like—why, I should laugh;
And if he, spying me, should fall to weep,
Beseech me to be good, repair his wrong,
Bid his poor leg smart less or grow again—
Well, as the chance were, this might take or else   90
Not take my fancy: I might hear his cry,
And give the manikin three sound legs for one,
Or pluck the other off, leave him like an egg,
And lessoned he was mine and merely clay.
Were this no pleasure, lying in the thyme,   95

[2] a bird with bright plumage

Drinking the mash, with brain become alive,
Making and marring clay at will? So He.

'Thinketh, such shows nor right nor wrong in Him,
Nor kind, nor cruel: He is strong and Lord.
'Am strong myself compared to yonder crabs   100
That march now from the mountain to the sea;
'Let twenty pass, and stone the twenty-first,
Loving not, hating not, just choosing so.
'Say, the first straggler that boasts purple spots
Shall join the file, one pincer twisted off;   105
'Say, this bruised fellow shall receive a worm,
And two worms he whose nippers end in red;
As it likes me each time, I do: so He.

Caliban, the speaker of this poem, is the misshappen evil-natured monster from Shakespeare's *The Tempest*. Here he lies in the dirt in a cave and contemplates what Setebos, his God, must be like. He decides that Setebos must, like himself, have to answer to a superior being, and that Setebos must react to things in the same way that Caliban himself does. How is this?

What does Caliban think was Setebos's reason for creating man? Why does he think so?

How would Caliban treat his creations if he were Setebos?

What does this poem suggest about man and his relationship to God?

What is the predominating meter of the poem? What function do variations in this meter have?

WARTY BLIGGENS THE TOAD

DON MARQUIS

i met a toad
the other day by the name
of warty bliggens
he was sitting under
a toadstool   5
feeling contented
he explained that when the cosmos

was created
that toadstool was especially
planned for his personal   10

shelter from sun and rain
thought out and prepared
for him

do not tell me
said warty bliggens   15
that there is not a purpose
in the universe
the thought is blasphemy

a little more
conversation revealed   20
that warty bliggens
considers himself to be
the center of the said
universe
the earth exists   25
to grow toadstools for him
to sit under
the sun to give him light
by day and the moon
and wheeling constellations   30
to make beautiful
the night for the sake of
warty bliggens

to what act of yours
do you impute   35
this interest on the part
of the creator
of the universe
i asked him
why is it that you   40
are so greatly favored

ask rather
said warty bliggens
what the universe
has done to deserve me   45
if i were a
human being i would
not laugh
too complacently
at poor warty bliggens   50
for similar

absurdities
have only too often
lodged in the crinkles
of the human cerebrum   55

What does warty bliggens represent?
Why is the lack of capital letters appropriate?
What does the poem say about man and his relationship to God?
Compare and contrast these ideas to those in "Caliban upon Setebos."

HUNGER

PETER DAVISON

Western gods are seldom fat:
Priests and painters see to that.
Christian men at grips with Mammon
Show their fealty by their famine.

Smiling Buddhas of the East,   5
Plump and padded from the feast,
Pensive, wonderful and wise,
Feed the hollow Buddhist's eyes.

Hungering Buddhist solves the test
If he sets his mind at rest   10
By the Way that Buddha set him:
"You, who love your god, forget him."

Yet, in matter Eucharistic,
Westerner is proved the mystic:
Though the mystery defeats him,   15
If he loves his God, he eats Him.

Define *Mammon, fealty, pensive, Eucharistic.*
What does this dissertation on the differences between Eastern and
Western gods say about man and religion in general?

AN TZU[1]

CATHERINE CHO WOO

To his students
   He seems so very tall
Teaching the doctrine of TAO
   Like thunder
He insisting   5
   "RIGHT ACTION!"

Above bare feet
   Among long hair and beards
      Or clean shaved faces
Young and old eyes   10
   Enlightened
      Listened with awed respect.

Under frosty long brows
   With penetrating vision
      Persuaded he: 15
"Pushing upwards![2]
   In order to attain modesty";[3]
"Practicing modesty!
   You will push upwards."

Peace   20
   Kindness
      Order
He is modeling his name.

One of the five books of the Confucian canon, I-Ching is the Book of Changes, which reflects the basic patterns of change which shape the world. It is traditionally ascribed to Wen Wang in the twelfth century BC.

[1] Master Anderson
[2] Hexagram 46 in the I-Ching
[3] Hexagram 15 in the I-Ching

MONGOL IN KRACOW

EVGENIJ VINOKUROV

(Translated by Vytas Dukas)

Upon the stones of churches, cawing,
A crow settles down, turning . . .
A Mongol, leaning on a spear,
Pensively looks at Kracow.
His face wrinkled, hairless,   5
Breaks into a smile . . .

. . . And bluish feet of Jesus
Pierced through by nails—
Centuries knew not of a more
Tormenting and mortal legend—   10
His face emerges from the thorns
Of a tragic wreath.

The Kracowites go to the cathedrals . . .
But the rider is obsessed by laughter,
The flowers shake and quiver   15
And naked is awakened turf.

He stops as if planted from a gallop
And becomes motionless.
On stretched out palms: There lies Europe—
Its villages and monasteries.   20

One sees strange things . . .
For the first and only time
The Mongol observed ominously
Europe through his slit eyes.

From the Pacific ocean,   25
As if they had an urge,
The horses snort damningly,
And Kibitdas[1] move in vapor.

Kracow is a city in southern Poland. In this poem we find juxtaposed East and West, Mongol and Christian, old and new. An analogy is drawn between Europe and Christ crucified. Why?

Comment on the images of this poem. How do they convey ideas?

[1] tilt-carts

A SMALL BOY IN CHURCH

ROBERT SHEPPARD

The floor was cold, grey stone.
The wooden seat felt hard against his own.
A simple child, he felt uneasy fear;
For God was here.
He looked around and guessed that God's retreat 5
Was hev'ning 'neath the rafters with the heat.
His eyes grown wide with wonderment and fear,
Strained hard to see through gloomy atmosphere.
His ears, though trained to hear the priest's command,
Collected words he did not understand, 10
And, though the voices 'round him said, "Rejoice"
He heard no joy ring in a single voice.

Each window, leaded, stained, admitted just
A gleam enough to light a stream of dust
Which flowed toward the floor, a frozen stare, 15
From leaded eyes of saints remembered there,
Of saints whose faces held eternal woe,
Who gazed upon the flock below.

The boy below could not but think it odd
That God, 20
    With all the stars of heaven 'neath his hand
    And every ocean's wave at his command
    All of the earth's great wooded lands to roam
Would choose to live in such a dismal home.

This poem expresses the feelings of a small boy in a large church.
What are his feelings? How real are they? How do diction and tone con-
tribute to their depiction?
What can we infer from the poem about man's relationship to God?

DIALOGUE AFTER BISHOP BERKELEY

JOHN HALL WHEELOCK

"You mean to say," I said,
"I made up the universe out of my head?"

"Sure," he said.

"I'm amazed," I said.

"Go on! You know it's so.   5
I know you know."

"What you mean?" I said.

"I mean like I said.
You made up the universe out of your head,
And maintain it still   10
By an act of will."

"You sure that's true?"

"Sure. All that worrying you do
Keeps the grass green and the sky blue."

"Gosh," I said,   15
"What'll happen when I die?"

"You won't have time to know I was right—
The whole damn thing'll go out like a light."

"You mean that?" I said.

"Sure," he said.   20
"Why don't you try?
It's nice to try."

Berkeley was an eighteenth century Irish bishop and philosopher who tried to reconcile Christianity with the science of his day. He said that "to exist" is "to be perceived." Hence, nothing exists unless it is perceived by some mind. His philosophy is called Idealism.
What do the final lines mean?

$$E = MC^2$$

MORRIS BISHOP

What was our trust, we trust not,
What was our faith, we doubt;

Whether we must or must not
  We may debate about.
The soul perhaps is a gust of gas   5
And wrong is a form of right—
But we know that Energy equals Mass
  By the Square of the Speed of Light.

What we have known, we know not,
  What we have proved, abjure.   10
Life is a tangled bow-knot,
  But one thing still is sure.
Come, little lad; come, little lass,
  Your docile creed recite:
"We know that Energy equals Mass   15
  By the Square of the Speed of Light."

This poem deals with the dichotomy of science and religion. What does it say about faith and knowledge? Why is the scientific formula called a creed? What does this suggest?

Notice the rhythm and meter of this poem. Why are they appropriate?

AGNOSTIC?

PAT FOLK

When for religion, man probes my soul,
I mock and tease with a blasphemous roll
  of my lilting tongue.
What man can't know, where man can't see,
Beneath the blarney-wrap of me,
I'm like a mole, a burrowing, seeking, half-blind mole.   5
The light is so very bright it blinds.
In fear of belief of such naked truth
That shines in bounteous wealth
Beamed for all kinds
I forswear, and search for life's reason in minds.   10
When the fire warms me, I don't ask why.
When bread satisfies me, I don't deny to eat
  And question rye or wheat,
But God is so much to try
Without searching   15
God is so much to try.
Truth is light and I'm half-blind.

And so, I delve the reversible dust,
Breathe through nostrils the breath I seek,
Travel deep roots, and trace   20
The life-green, questioning shoots
Up to the blinding light.

Define *agnostic*. How does an agnostic differ from an atheist? Is the speaker an agnostic?

Where does he search for God? Why? What does he mean in lines eighteen through twenty-two?

KID STUFF

December 1942

FRANK HORNE

The wise guys
tell me
that Christmas
is Kid Stuff . . .
Maybe they've got   5
something there—
Two thousand years ago
three wise guys
chased a star
across a continent   10
to bring
frankincense and myrrh
to a Kid
born in a manger
with an idea in his head . . .   15

And as the bombs
crash
all over the world
today
the real wise guys   20
know
that we've all
got to go chasing stars
again
in the hope   25
that we can get back
some of that

*Kids stuff
born two thousand years ago*
183

Kid Stuff
born two thousand years ago.

How do the phrases "wise guys" and "Kid Stuff" change?
How do you visualize the speaker of this poem?
The poem was written during World War II. Has its significance
diminished?

FLOWER IN THE CRANNIED WALL

ALFRED, LORD TENNYSON

Flower in the crannied wall,
I pluck you out of the crannies,
I hold you here, root and all, in my hand,
Little flower—but *if* I could understand
What you are, root and all, and all in all,   5
I should know what God and man is.

Why is *if* italicized?
Why does the speaker feel that he would understand God and man
if he understood the flower? What does this tell us about man's relation-
ship to God?

YET DO I MARVEL

COUNTEE CULLEN

I doubt not God is good, well-meaning, kind,
And did He stoop to quibble could tell why
The little buried mole continues blind,
Why flesh that mirrors Him must someday die,
Make plain the reason tortured Tantalus   5
Is baited by the fickle fruit, declare
If merely brute caprice dooms Sisyphus
To struggle up a never-ending stair.
Inscrutable His ways are, and immune
To catechism by a mind too strewn   10
With petty cares to slightly understand
What awful brain compels His awful hand.

Yet do I marvel at this curious thing:
To make a poet black, and bid him sing!

What do the mole, mortal man, Tantalus, Sisyphus, and the black
poet have in common? What is the speaker suggesting?
Define *inscrutable* and *catechism.*
In what sense is *awful* used?

HEAVEN

RUPERT BROOKE

Fish (fly-replete, in depth of June,
Dawdling away their wat'ry noon)
Ponder deep wisdom, dark or clear,
Each secret fishy hope or fear.
Fish say, they have their Stream and Pond;   5
But is there anything Beyond?
This life cannot be All, they swear,
For how unpleasant, if it were!
One may not doubt that, somehow, Good
Shall come of Water and of Mud;   10
And, sure, the reverent eye must see
A Purpose in Liquidity.
We darkly know, by Faith we cry,
The future is not Wholly Dry.
Mud unto mud!—Death eddies near—   15
Not here the appointed End, not here!
But somewhere, beyond Space and Time,
Is wetter water, slimier slime!
And there (they trust) there swimmeth One
Who swam ere rivers were begun,   20
Immense, of fishy form and mind,
Squamous, omnipotent, and kind;
And under that Almighty Fin,
The littlest fish may enter in.
Oh! never fly conceals a hook,   25
Fish say, in the Eternal Brook,
But more than mundane weeds are there,
And mud, celestially fair;
Fat caterpillars drift around,
And Paradisal grubs are found;   30
Unfading moths, immortal flies,

And the worm that never dies.
And in that Heaven of all their wish,
There shall be no more land, say fish.

This poem gives a fish-eye view of heaven. Describe this vision and compare it with man's usual view of heaven. What does the poem suggest about man?
Define *squamous, omnipotent, mundane, replete.*
Why are the closed couplets appropriate? Why are so many words capitalized? What do sound patterns add to the poem?

A THEOLOGICAL DEFINITION

GEORGE OPPEN

A small room, the varnished floor
Making an L around the bed,

What is or is true as
Happiness

Windows opening on the sea,   5
The green painted railings of the balcony
Against the rock, the bushes and the sea running

How is the title related to the poem?
What images are evoked? What do they suggest?
What is "Happiness"?

THE SECOND COMING

WILLIAM BUTLER YEATS

Turning and turning in the widening gyre
The falcon cannot hear the falconer;
Things fall apart; the center cannot hold;
Mere anarchy is loosed upon the world,
The blood-dimmed tide is loosed, and everywhere   5
The ceremony of innocence is drowned;
The best lack all conviction, while the worst
Are full of passionate intensity.

Surely some revelation is at hand;
Surely the Second Coming is at hand.   10
The Second Coming! Hardly are those words out
When a vast image out of *Spiritus Mundi*
Troubles my sight: somewhere in sands of the desert
A shape with lion body and the head of a man,
A gaze blank and pitiless as the sun,   15
Is moving its slow thighs, while all about it
Reel shadows of the indignant desert birds.
The darkness drops again; but now I know
That twenty centuries of stony sleep
Were vexed to nightmare by a rocking cradle,   20
And what rough beast, its hour come round at last,
Slouches towards Bethlehem to be born?

Define *gyre*.

Yeats believed that one kind of historical age would be replaced by its opposite every two thousand years. This poem was written in 1919. He felt that World War I heralded the end of the Christian age and the beginning of a new one. To what does the Second Coming refer in Christianity?

Spiritus Mundi means world spirit—the collective unconscious of mankind.

What relationship do the falcon and falconer have to one another? What do they symbolize?

To what does the "blood-dimmed tide" probably refer? The "ceremony of innocence"? The "shape with lion body and the head of a man"? The "rocking cradle"? The "rough beast"?

Notice how the first stanza moves from concrete imagery to abstraction, while the second stanza moves in the opposite direction. What does this progression suggest in relationship to the theme?

Compare the last fourteen lines to Shelley's "Ozymandias" (page 138).

Notice the rhythm and meter of the poem. How do they work with the theme?

THEY WERE PUTTING UP THE STATUE

LAWRENCE FERLINGHETTI

They were putting up the statue
  of Saint Francis
    in front of the church
      of Saint Francis

           in the city of San Francisco   5
in a little side street
           just off the Avenue
                 where no birds sang
  and the sun was coming up on time
                 in its usual fashion   10
    and just beginning to shine
             on the statue of Saint Francis
    where no birds sang
And a lot of old Italians
           were standing all around   15
    in the little side street
           just off the Avenue
    watching the wily workers
             who were hoisting up the statue
with a chain and a crane   20
           and other implements
And a lot of young reporters
           in button-down clothes
were taking down the words
           of one young priest   25
  who was propping up the statue
           with all his arguments

    And all the while
           while no birds sang
              any Saint Francis Passion   30
and while the lookers kept looking
           up at Saint Francis
  with his arms outstretched
           to the birds which weren't there
a very tall and very purely naked   35
           young virgin
with very long and very straight
           straw hair
  and wearing only a very small
           bird's nest   40
    in a very existential place
           kept passing thru the crowd
              all the while
    and up and down the steps
           in front of Saint Francis   45
  her eyes downcast all the while
           and singing to herself

How is the priest propping up the statue? What does this suggest?
Why don't the birds sing? Why is this significant?
What does the virgin suggest? Is it important that she sings to herself?
That her eyes are downcast?
Saint Francis, who founded the Franciscan Order, lived in extreme
austerity.

JAN HUS

EVGENIJ VINOKUROV

(Translated by Vytas Dukas)

He was humble and wise
And he respected sanctity,
And could express himself best of all
In Golden Latin.
None would guess in him   5
Even with candles in daytime
A titan:
A humble cowl,
And a humble soutane.
He could have lived a hundred years, but once   10
He, in passion invincible,
Shook his bony arm
On the church yard.
And you could hear miles away,
How instead of clerical rules,   15
He praised the simplicity of the apostles.
. . . Into the fire went this wise Czech . . .

The universe exclaimed:
"What is it that you want my man?!
What is it that you lack?"   20

Define *titan, soutane, invincible.*
Jan Hus was a fourteenth century religious reformer who was labeled
a heretic and burned at the stake. Why is he said to speak in "Golden"
Latin?
How is Hus depicted here? How does the speaker feel about him?

THE CRUCIFIX

AUGUSTINE BOWE

They came. Well, yes, they came,
As I had always thought they would,
But over and over they said the same
Words, because they thought they should,
To me nailed here in public shame.   5
Have you ever tried to hold the attention of a child?
Being God is something like that, if you take it seriously.
The guilty ones are too meek and mild,
The earnest ones behave deliriously.
I wanted them to be gently wild.   10

Perhaps the priests are right to give them beads
To tell, invent monotonous response
To endless litanies. They know their needs.
If they came unrehearsed and saw me all at once,
They would run madly off among the weeds.   15

Who is the speaker? What does he mean by line ten? By lines fourteen
and fifteen?
How do you interpret the final stanza?
What point is made about God and about man?
What figurative language is used?

THE PULLEY

GEORGE HERBERT

When God at first made man,
Having a glass of blessings standing by,
"Let us," said he, "pour on him all we can.
Let the world's riches, which disperséd lie,
Contract into a span."   5

So strength first made a way;
Then beauty flowed, then wisdom, honor, pleasure.
When almost all was out, God made a stay,
Perceiving that, alone of all his treasure,
Rest in the bottom lay.   10

"For if I should," said he,
"Bestow this jewel also on my creature,
He would adore my gifts instead of me,
And rest in Nature, not the God of Nature;
So both should losers be.   15

"Yet let him keep the rest,
But keep them with repining restlessness.
Let him be rich and weary, that at least,
If goodness lead him not, yet weariness
May toss him to my breast."   20

To what does the title refer?
In what senses is *rest* used?
How many speakers are there?
What is the central purpose of the poem? "The Pulley" was written
early in the seventeenth century. It may have implications today that
Herbert never dreamed of. What might they be?

HOLY SONNET

JOHN DONNE

14

Batter my heart, three-personed God; for You
As yet but knock, breathe, shine, and seek to mend;
That I may rise and stand, o'erthrow me, and bend
Your force to break, blow, burn, and make me new.
I, like an usurped town, to another due,
Labor to admit You, but O, to no end;
Reason, Your viceroy in me, me should defend,
But is captived, and proves weak or untrue.
Yet dearly I love You, and would be loved fain,
But am betrothed unto Your enemy.   10
Divorce me, untie or break that knot again;
Take me to You, imprison me, for I,
Except You enthrall me, never shall be free,
Nor ever chaste, except You ravish me.

Donne speaks to God as if to a lover. In "The Canonization" he spoke
to his lover as if to God (see page 52). Is he being sacrilegious? (Donne
was a clergyman during the seventeenth century, like George Herbert.)
What do you make of the last four lines?

UNTITLED

SHARON BUCK

God said if you would not love me,
He would.
He wouldn't tell me
where to kneel.

What kind of God is pictured in this poem? What specifically implies
this? Can this poem be interpreted in more than one way?

Index of Titles and Poets

Index of Titles and Poets

Sheppard, Robert: *A Small Boy in Church*, 180
Small Boy in Church, A, Sheppard, 180
Sosna, Sharon: *The Soul of Youth—The Fear of Age*, from, 96
Soul of Youth—The Fear of Age, The, from, Sosna, 96
Southern Mansion, Bontemps, 86
Spencer, Anne: *Letter to My Sister*, 57
Stahl, D. A.: *Time Past*, 3
Stevens, Wallace: *The Common Life*, 80; *The Man with the Blue Guitar*, from, 166–68; *Peter Quince at the Clavier*, 160
Story of Isaac, The, Cohen, 82
Suckling, Sir John: *Out Upon It!*, 107
Survival: Infantry, Oppen, 128

T

The Tag, Almon, 152
Telepathy to Someone Special or Invasion, Allen, 45
Tennyson, Alfred, Lord: *The Eagle*, 142; *Flower in the Crannied Wall*, 184
Theological Definition, A, Oppen, 186
There Are Many Trades, Vinokurov (trans. Vytas Dukas), 79
These Lives, Shapiro, 25
They Were Putting Up the Statue, Ferlinghetti, 187
Time Past, Stahl, 3
To a Mad Friend, Davison, 24
To Autumn, Keats, 101
To His Coy Mistress, Marvell, 50
To My Mother, Barker, 73
To Smith, Miles, 26
Treehouse, The, Emanuel, 28

U

Untitled ("God said if you would not love me"), Buck, 192
Untitled ("I'M DEAD"), Buck, 145
Untitled ("I think it was because you laughed"), Buck, 58
Untitled, Pogliano, 21

V

Valediction: Forbidding Mourning, A, Donne, 66
Viewpoints, Murray, 5

Vinokurov, Evgenij: *Jan Hus*, 189; *Mongol in Kracow*, 179; *Past Midnight*, 11; *There Are Many Trades*, 79

W

Walking, Richards, 27
War Is Here, The, Allen, 122
War—Last Year in June, This Year, The, Weber, 130
Warning, The, Creeley, 54
warty bliggens the toad, Marquis, 175
Waste Land, The, from ("At the violet hour"), Eliot, 64
Waste Land, The, from ("The chair she sat in"), Eliot, 110
Weaver, Miles: *The End*, 126
Weber, Alfred K.: *Father's Face*, 152; *From Pigeons to People*, 93; *The War—Last Year in June, This Year*, 130
Wheelock, John Hall: *The Big I*, 23; *Colloquy*, 146; *Dialogue after Bishop Berkeley*, 180; *Earth*, 108
When a Man Hath No Freedom, Byron, 114
When Sometimes, Denman, 8
While My Guitar Gently Weeps, Harrison, 97
Who Killed Davey Moore?, Dylan, 154
Wilbur, Richard: *A Fire-Truck*, 95
Williams, William Carlos: *A Cold Front*, 75; *Death*, 145; *Picture of a Nude in a Machine Shop*, 46
With God on Our Side, Dylan, 115
Wolfe, Thomas, *Niggertown*, 87
Woman, Goldsmith, 65
Woman, Pound, 40
Woo, Catherine Cho: *An Tzu*, 178; *Memories*, 59
Wordsworth, William, *The World Is Too Much with Us*, 93
World Is Too Much with Us, The, Wordsworth, 93

Y

Yeats, William Butler: *Leda and the Swan*, 109; *Long-Legged Fly*, 98; *The Second Coming*, 186
Yesterday, Pogliano, 58
Yet Do I Marvel, Cullen, 184

197

Index of Topics